Hybrid Cloud Strategies

Integrating On-Premises Infrastructure with Cloud Solutions Effectively

Greyson Chesterfield

COPYRIGHT

DISCLAIMER

The information provided in this book is for general informational purposes only. All content in this book reflects the author's views and is based on their research, knowledge, and experiences. The author and publisher make no representations or warranties of any kind concerning the completeness, accuracy, reliability, suitability, or availability of the information contained herein.

This book is not intended to be a substitute for professional advice, diagnosis, or treatment. Readers should seek professional advice for any specific concerns or conditions. The author and publisher disclaim any liability or responsibility for any direct, indirect, incidental, or consequential loss or damage arising from the use of the information contained in this book.

Contents

Introduction

The rapid evolution of technology has ushered in an era where flexibility, scalability, and efficiency are no longer luxuries but necessities for organizations striving to remain competitive. In this dynamic landscape, **hybrid cloud computing** has emerged as a transformative solution, bridging the gap between traditional on-premises systems and the vast capabilities of public and private cloud platforms. This book, *Mastering Hybrid Cloud: Strategies, Challenges, and Practical Solutions*, is designed to equip readers with the knowledge, skills, and tools needed to navigate and succeed in the hybrid cloud era.

Why Hybrid Cloud Matters

Hybrid cloud is not just a technological framework; it's a strategic enabler for innovation and growth. By combining the control and security of on-premises systems with the flexibility and scalability of the cloud, hybrid cloud offers the best of both worlds. Organizations can optimize resources, enhance operational efficiency, and meet complex compliance requirements while retaining the ability to innovate at scale.

Key Advantages of Hybrid Cloud:

1. **Flexibility:** Dynamically allocate resources to meet changing demands.

2. **Cost Optimization:** Strategically use on-premises systems for predictable workloads and cloud resources for variable demands.

3. **Enhanced Security:** Maintain control over sensitive data while leveraging cloud capabilities.

4. **Innovation Enablement:** Utilize advanced cloud-native tools like AI, machine learning, and big data analytics.

Despite its benefits, adopting and managing hybrid cloud environments is not without challenges. Integration complexities, security concerns, and skill gaps often create hurdles for organizations. This book addresses these challenges head-on, providing actionable insights and practical guidance.

Who This Book Is For

This book caters to a diverse audience, making it a valuable resource for:

- **IT Professionals:** Gain in-depth knowledge of hybrid cloud architectures, tools, and best practices.

- **Business Leaders:** Understand how hybrid cloud strategies align with organizational goals.

- **Students and Learners:** Build a strong foundation in hybrid cloud concepts and practical applications.

- **Hobbyists and Enthusiasts:** Explore the possibilities of hybrid cloud technology through hands-on projects and tutorials.

Whether you are new to hybrid cloud computing or seeking to deepen your expertise, this book provides a structured pathway to success.

What You'll Learn

Hybrid cloud is a multi-faceted domain encompassing architecture, strategy, security, cost management, and more. This book is structured to guide you through the journey, from foundational concepts to advanced implementations, with real-world applications and hands-on tutorials.

Key Themes Explored

1. Foundational Concepts:
The book begins by defining hybrid cloud and its components, exploring why organizations choose this approach, and examining its benefits and challenges. Readers will gain a clear understanding of how hybrid cloud environments operate and how they differ from other models like public and private clouds.

2. Planning and Strategy:
A successful hybrid cloud implementation starts with a solid plan. Chapters on assessing existing infrastructure, setting goals, and creating migration roadmaps provide a strategic framework for organizations.

3. Practical Implementation:
Step-by-step tutorials and projects bring hybrid cloud concepts to life. From setting up demo environments to building CI/CD pipelines, these chapters offer hands-on experience to bridge the gap between theory and practice.

4. Advanced Topics:
Emerging technologies like AI, edge computing, and quantum computing are transforming hybrid cloud environments. The book delves into how these advancements are shaping the future and how organizations can prepare to leverage them effectively.

5. Real-World Applications and Case Studies:
Practical insights from industries such as healthcare, finance, and manufacturing showcase how hybrid cloud solutions are solving real-world problems and driving innovation.

6. Troubleshooting and Optimization:
Hybrid cloud environments come with their share of challenges. Chapters on debugging, performance optimization, and cost management provide the tools and strategies needed to tackle common issues effectively.

Structure of the Book

The book is organized into 20 chapters, each building upon the previous to create a cohesive narrative:

1. **Introduction to Hybrid Cloud:** Foundations, benefits, and challenges.

2. **Understanding On-Premises Infrastructure:** The traditional systems that hybrid cloud integrates with.

3. **Cloud Computing Basics:** The models and services shaping cloud technology.

4. **Why Choose a Hybrid Cloud Strategy?** Exploring the strategic advantages.

5. **Planning a Hybrid Cloud Implementation:** Setting goals and creating a migration roadmap.

6. **Architecture of Hybrid Cloud Solutions:** Designing resilient and scalable hybrid setups.

7. **Networking for Hybrid Cloud Environments:** Building secure and efficient connectivity.

8. **Data Management in Hybrid Cloud:** Synchronization, governance, and backup strategies.

9. **Security in Hybrid Cloud Solutions:** Protecting resources and ensuring compliance.

10. **Workload Distribution and Optimization:** Deciding where workloads should reside.

11.**Automation in Hybrid Cloud:** Streamlining processes with tools and techniques.

12.**Monitoring and Analytics:** Gaining visibility into hybrid environments.

13.**Real-World Applications of Hybrid Cloud:** Industry use cases and success stories.

14.**Managing Hybrid Cloud Costs:** Strategies for cost efficiency and optimization.

15.**Addressing Challenges in Hybrid Cloud Adoption:** Overcoming resistance, skill gaps, and integration pitfalls.

16.**Regulatory and Compliance Considerations:** Navigating GDPR, HIPAA, and industry standards.

17.**Future Trends in Hybrid Cloud Technology:** AI, edge computing, and quantum advancements.

18.**Hands-On Tutorials and Projects:** Practical guides to hybrid cloud implementation.

19.**Troubleshooting Hybrid Cloud Issues:** Debugging and resolving common challenges.

20.**Conclusion and Next Steps:** Reflecting on lessons learned and future opportunities.

What Makes This Book Unique?

1. **Comprehensive Coverage:** From beginner-friendly introductions to advanced technical discussions, this book covers every aspect of hybrid cloud computing.

2. **Actionable Insights:** Each chapter provides practical guidance that can be directly applied to real-world scenarios.

3. **Hands-On Focus:** Tutorials and projects ensure readers gain practical experience alongside theoretical knowledge.

4. **Future-Focused:** The book not only addresses current challenges but also explores how emerging technologies will shape hybrid cloud environments.

Why Hybrid Cloud Is the Future

As businesses strive to stay competitive in an ever-changing world, hybrid cloud computing offers a path to agility and innovation. It is not merely a technological choice but a strategic imperative, allowing organizations to:

- Scale seamlessly while maintaining control over critical data.

- Innovate rapidly by leveraging cloud-native tools and services.

- Adapt to new challenges and opportunities with resilience.

Hybrid cloud aligns with the realities of today's IT needs, making it an essential component of future-ready strategies.

How to Get the Most Out of This Book

To maximize the value of this book:

1. **Follow the Tutorials:** Practical exercises provide a hands-on understanding of hybrid cloud implementations.

2. **Apply What You Learn:** Use the concepts and strategies discussed to design and optimize your hybrid cloud environment.

3. **Stay Curious:** Explore additional resources and emerging trends to deepen your knowledge.

4. **Collaborate and Share:** Engage with the hybrid cloud community to exchange ideas and solutions.

Final Thoughts

This book is more than a guide; it's a roadmap to mastering hybrid cloud technology. Whether you are building your first hybrid cloud environment or optimizing an existing strategy, the knowledge and insights provided here will empower you to succeed.

Hybrid cloud is not just about technology—it's about transformation. By embracing this approach, organizations and individuals alike can unlock new levels of efficiency, innovation, and opportunity.

Your journey into the hybrid cloud era begins here. Let's build the future together.

Chapter 1: Introduction to Hybrid Cloud

Understanding Hybrid Cloud

Hybrid cloud is a computing environment that combines the capabilities of on-premises infrastructure with public and private cloud services. This integration allows organizations to seamlessly manage and scale workloads across multiple platforms while optimizing for performance, cost, and security. Unlike purely on-premises or fully cloud-based solutions, hybrid cloud strategies offer a balanced approach to modern IT challenges, empowering businesses to tailor their technology stack to meet unique needs.

Components of Hybrid Cloud

To understand hybrid cloud, it's essential to break down its core components:

1. **On-Premises Infrastructure**
   Traditional IT infrastructure that resides within an organization's data centers forms the backbone of hybrid cloud environments. This includes physical servers, storage devices, and networking equipment. On-

premises systems are often utilized for sensitive workloads requiring strict data control or regulatory compliance.

2. **Public Cloud**
Public cloud services, provided by companies like AWS, Microsoft Azure, and Google Cloud, deliver scalable and flexible computing resources over the internet. These services often include Infrastructure as a Service (IaaS), Platform as a Service (PaaS), and Software as a Service (SaaS). Public clouds are ideal for handling fluctuating workloads and enabling innovation without large upfront investments.

3. **Private Cloud**
Private cloud environments are dedicated to a single organization, offering greater control and customization compared to public clouds. These clouds can reside on-premises or be hosted by third-party providers. They are typically used for workloads that require enhanced security and performance.

4. **Integration and Connectivity Tools**
The glue of hybrid cloud strategies is the suite of integration tools that enable communication between on-premises and

cloud environments. These include APIs, gateways, and hybrid cloud platforms that ensure data and applications move seamlessly across systems.

Benefits of Hybrid Cloud Adoption

Hybrid cloud adoption offers numerous advantages, making it an attractive option for organizations navigating the complexities of modern IT. Below are some of the most significant benefits:

1. **Flexibility and Scalability**
   Hybrid cloud solutions provide unparalleled flexibility, allowing organizations to scale their computing resources as needed. For instance, during peak business periods, workloads can be offloaded to public cloud resources to handle increased demand without overburdening on-premises infrastructure.

2. **Cost Optimization**
   By leveraging public clouds for non-sensitive or temporary workloads, organizations can reduce the need for costly on-premises hardware. Hybrid clouds also allow

businesses to adopt a pay-as-you-go model, reducing capital expenditures.

3. **Enhanced Security and Compliance**
For industries with stringent regulatory requirements, hybrid cloud offers a way to maintain control over sensitive data by keeping it on-premises while still benefiting from the scalability of the cloud. This dual approach ensures compliance without sacrificing innovation.

4. **Business Continuity and Disaster Recovery**
Hybrid cloud environments support robust disaster recovery strategies by providing redundant storage and backup capabilities. In the event of an on-premises failure, workloads can shift to the cloud, ensuring business continuity.

5. **Support for Legacy Systems**
Many organizations have legacy applications that are difficult or impractical to migrate fully to the cloud. Hybrid cloud allows these systems to coexist with modern cloud-native applications, ensuring smooth operations without costly overhauls.

6. **Accelerated Innovation**
Hybrid cloud environments empower

organizations to experiment with emerging technologies like AI, machine learning, and big data analytics. Public clouds provide access to cutting-edge tools and services, enabling rapid development and deployment.

Challenges of Hybrid Cloud Adoption

While the benefits of hybrid cloud are compelling, organizations must address several challenges to achieve a seamless implementation:

1. **Complex Integration**
   Integrating on-premises systems with cloud platforms can be technically challenging. Compatibility issues between legacy infrastructure and modern cloud services often require extensive customization and expertise.

2. **Security and Compliance Risks**
   Managing security across multiple environments is a complex task. Organizations must ensure consistent security policies and implement robust identity and access management (IAM) solutions to prevent unauthorized access.

3. **Cost Management**

   Hybrid cloud environments can lead to unexpected costs if not carefully monitored. The pay-as-you-go model of public clouds, combined with on-premises maintenance costs, requires diligent tracking to avoid budget overruns.

4. **Skill Gaps**

   Adopting a hybrid cloud strategy often necessitates specialized skills that may not exist within an organization. IT teams must be trained in cloud technologies and hybrid infrastructure management to ensure smooth operations.

5. **Latency and Performance Issues**

   Data transfer between on-premises and cloud systems can introduce latency, impacting application performance. Optimizing network connectivity and deploying edge computing solutions can help mitigate these issues.

Key Drivers for Hybrid Cloud Adoption

Organizations are increasingly turning to hybrid cloud strategies for a variety of reasons, driven by both internal needs and external market forces:

1. **Digital Transformation**
   As businesses seek to modernize their operations, hybrid cloud provides a pathway to embrace digital transformation. By combining legacy systems with cloud-native applications, organizations can enhance agility without disrupting core functions.

2. **Industry-Specific Requirements**
   Some industries, such as healthcare and finance, face strict regulatory requirements regarding data privacy and security. Hybrid cloud allows these organizations to store sensitive data on-premises while leveraging the cloud for less critical operations.

3. **Globalization and Remote Work**
   The rise of remote work and global operations has increased the need for flexible and accessible IT solutions. Hybrid cloud enables employees and teams to access resources and collaborate seamlessly across geographies.

4. **Competitive Pressure**
   To stay competitive, businesses must adopt innovative technologies that improve efficiency and customer experiences. Hybrid cloud enables rapid experimentation and deployment of new solutions, ensuring companies remain agile in dynamic markets.

5. **Sustainability Goals**
   Many organizations are prioritizing sustainability and energy efficiency in their IT strategies. Hybrid cloud solutions allow businesses to reduce their environmental footprint by optimizing resource usage and consolidating workloads.

6. **Emerging Technologies**
   The hybrid cloud is an enabler for emerging technologies such as edge computing and the Internet of Things (IoT). These technologies benefit from the proximity of on-premises infrastructure while leveraging cloud resources for advanced analytics.

The Journey Ahead

The hybrid cloud represents a paradigm shift in how organizations approach IT infrastructure and services. By blending the best of on-premises and cloud environments, businesses can create a tailored solution that aligns with their unique goals and challenges. However, realizing the full potential of hybrid cloud requires a clear strategy, robust planning, and a commitment to continuous improvement.

In the chapters that follow, we will explore the intricacies of hybrid cloud integration, providing actionable insights and practical guidance to help you navigate this complex yet rewarding landscape. From architecture design and data management to security and real-world applications, this guide aims to equip you with the knowledge and tools needed to succeed in your hybrid cloud journey.

Chapter 2: Understanding On-Premises Infrastructure

In the rapidly evolving world of IT, the role of on-premises infrastructure remains integral to many organizations. Even as cloud solutions gain widespread adoption, on-premises systems continue to offer distinct advantages for specific use cases. This chapter delves into the foundations of traditional IT infrastructure, explores its core components, and evaluates its benefits and drawbacks.

Overview of Traditional IT Infrastructure

Traditional IT infrastructure refers to the hardware, software, and networking resources that organizations deploy and manage within their own facilities. These systems are typically located in data centers owned and operated by the organization, ensuring complete control over physical and digital resources.

Before the advent of cloud computing, on-premises infrastructure was the dominant model for powering business operations. While cloud platforms have transformed the IT landscape, on-premises systems remain a viable choice for many organizations due to their reliability, customization, and security.

Key Features of Traditional IT Infrastructure:

- **Physical Presence:** All resources are physically located within the organization's facilities, allowing for direct oversight and control.

- **Customization:** Organizations can tailor hardware and software to meet specific operational requirements.

- **Data Sovereignty:** Data remains within the organization's boundaries, which is critical for industries with strict regulatory requirements.

- **Maintenance Responsibility:** IT teams are responsible for the upkeep, security, and upgrades of all resources.

Core Components of On-Premises Infrastructure

On-premises systems comprise several critical components that work together to support business operations. Each component plays a specific role in ensuring efficient and secure IT services.

1. Servers

Servers are the backbone of on-premises infrastructure, providing the computational power required to run applications, process data, and deliver services.

Types of Servers:

- **Application Servers:** Host and run business applications, such as ERP, CRM, and databases.

- **Web Servers:** Deliver web pages and manage internet traffic.

- **File Servers:** Store and manage access to files and documents.

- **Database Servers:** Provide storage and processing power for database management systems.

Modern servers can be physical or virtual. Virtualization technologies allow multiple virtual servers to run on a single physical machine, optimizing resource utilization and flexibility.

2. Storage

Storage systems in on-premises infrastructure are responsible for housing data securely and reliably.

Types of On-Premises Storage:

- **Direct-Attached Storage (DAS):** Storage devices directly connected to a server, offering simplicity but limited scalability.

- **Network-Attached Storage (NAS):** Centralized storage accessible over a network, ideal for file sharing and backups.

- **Storage Area Network (SAN):** High-performance storage systems designed for mission-critical applications, such as databases and large-scale analytics.

Organizations may also implement backup and archival solutions to protect against data loss and ensure compliance with retention policies.

3. Networking

Networking infrastructure connects all components of the IT environment, enabling communication and data exchange.

Key Networking Components:

- **Routers and Switches:** Direct data traffic between devices and networks.

- **Firewalls:** Protect the network from unauthorized access and cyberattacks.

- **Load Balancers:** Distribute incoming traffic across servers to optimize performance and prevent overload.

- **Network Cabling and Wireless Access Points:** Facilitate physical and wireless connections between devices.

A well-designed network is crucial for ensuring reliable and efficient operations, particularly in complex enterprise environments.

4. Software

On-premises systems require a range of software solutions to manage hardware resources, run applications, and secure data.

Types of Software in On-Premises Infrastructure:

- **Operating Systems (OS):** Manage hardware resources and provide a platform for applications (e.g., Windows Server, Linux).

- **Enterprise Applications:** Power business functions such as HR, finance, and customer relationship management.

- **Security Software:** Includes antivirus, intrusion detection systems (IDS), and encryption tools.

- **Management Tools:** Monitor and control IT infrastructure, such as virtualization platforms and network monitoring tools.

The software stack is customized to align with the organization's goals and regulatory requirements, offering flexibility but increasing complexity.

Pros of On-Premises Systems

On-premises infrastructure offers a range of advantages that make it the preferred choice for certain organizations and scenarios:

1. Control and Customization

Organizations have complete control over their infrastructure, enabling them to customize hardware and software configurations to meet specific business needs. This control is especially valuable for industries with unique operational requirements.

2. Data Security and Privacy

Sensitive data can be stored and processed on-site, reducing the risk of unauthorized access or data breaches. This level of security is critical for sectors such as healthcare, finance, and government.

3. Regulatory Compliance

Many regulatory frameworks require organizations to maintain strict control over data location and access. On-premises infrastructure ensures compliance with data sovereignty and industry-specific mandates.

4. Low Latency and High Performance

With resources located physically close to end-users and applications, on-premises systems deliver low-latency performance. This is vital for time-sensitive applications, such as real-time analytics and manufacturing systems.

5. Independence from Third-Party Providers

On-premises infrastructure eliminates reliance on external service providers, reducing risks associated with vendor lock-in, service outages, or price increases.

6. Predictable Costs

While on-premises systems require significant upfront investments, operational costs can be predictable over time. Organizations have greater control over budgeting and resource allocation.

Cons of On-Premises Systems

Despite their benefits, on-premises systems also come with notable challenges and limitations:

1. High Initial Costs

Deploying on-premises infrastructure requires substantial capital investment in hardware, software, and facilities. This can be a barrier for smaller organizations with limited budgets.

2. Maintenance and Upkeep

Organizations are responsible for the maintenance, upgrades, and security of their infrastructure. This includes patching software, replacing hardware, and managing network performance, which can strain IT resources.

3. Scalability Limitations

Scaling on-premises systems to accommodate growth requires significant planning and investment. Unlike cloud solutions, on-premises infrastructure cannot be scaled up or down on demand.

4. Disaster Recovery Challenges

In the event of a natural disaster, power outage, or hardware failure, on-premises systems may face prolonged downtime unless robust backup and recovery systems are in place.

5. Resource Intensity

Managing on-premises infrastructure demands skilled personnel, dedicated space, and energy resources. This increases operational complexity and environmental impact.

6. Slower Innovation Cycles

Upgrading on-premises systems to adopt new technologies can be a slow and expensive process. This may hinder an organization's ability to innovate and stay competitive in fast-paced industries.

On-Premises Systems in a Hybrid World

While the rise of cloud computing has led many organizations to migrate workloads to the cloud, on-premises systems continue to play a critical role in hybrid IT environments. By integrating on-premises infrastructure with cloud solutions, businesses can leverage the strengths of both models.

For example, sensitive data and mission-critical applications can remain on-premises for enhanced security, while non-sensitive workloads are offloaded to the cloud to take advantage of scalability and cost savings.

Key Considerations for Hybrid Integration:

- **Interoperability:** Ensuring seamless communication between on-premises and cloud environments.

- **Security:** Implementing consistent security policies across both systems.

- **Workload Distribution:** Deciding which workloads are best suited for on-premises vs. cloud deployment.

Understanding on-premises infrastructure is essential for grasping the broader landscape of modern IT systems. While the cloud has revolutionized the way businesses operate, traditional on-premises systems offer unique advantages in terms of control, security, and performance.

As organizations continue to navigate the challenges of digital transformation, the ability to integrate on-premises and cloud environments will be a key driver of success. By leveraging the strengths of each model, businesses can build a flexible and resilient IT foundation that meets the demands of today's dynamic marketplace.

Chapter 3: Cloud Computing Basics

Cloud computing has become the cornerstone of modern IT infrastructure, enabling businesses to access computing resources on-demand without the need for extensive on-premises hardware. This chapter introduces the foundational concepts of cloud computing, exploring the distinctions between public, private, and hybrid clouds, examining the core service models (IaaS, PaaS, and SaaS), and detailing the offerings of major cloud providers.

Understanding Cloud Computing

At its core, cloud computing refers to the delivery of computing services—such as servers, storage, databases, networking, software, and analytics—over the internet ("the cloud"). It eliminates the need for organizations to own and maintain physical hardware, offering scalability, flexibility, and cost-efficiency.

Key characteristics of cloud computing include:

- **On-Demand Availability:** Resources can be accessed whenever needed.

- **Scalability:** Systems can be scaled up or down to meet fluctuating demands.

- **Pay-as-You-Go Pricing:** Organizations only pay for the resources they use.

- **Global Access:** Cloud services can be accessed from anywhere with an internet connection.

Public, Private, and Hybrid Clouds: Differences and Use Cases

Cloud environments are categorized based on their deployment model. Each model has unique attributes suited to specific business needs.

1. Public Cloud

Definition:
A public cloud is a shared environment where resources are owned and managed by a third-party cloud provider. Customers access these resources over the internet, typically through a subscription or pay-as-you-go model.

Key Features:

- Multi-tenancy, with resources shared among multiple organizations.

- High scalability and flexibility.

- No need for capital investment in hardware.

Advantages:

- **Cost Efficiency:** No upfront infrastructure costs; suitable for startups and SMEs.

- **Scalability:** Resources can be added instantly to meet growing demands.

- **Global Reach:** Cloud providers offer data centers worldwide for low-latency access.

Challenges:

- Limited control over infrastructure.

- Potential security concerns due to shared environments.

Use Cases:

- Hosting websites and blogs.

- Running development and testing environments.

- Big data analytics.

2. Private Cloud

Definition:
A private cloud is a dedicated environment designed for a single organization. It can be hosted on-premises or by a third-party provider but remains isolated from other customers.

Key Features:

- Single-tenancy for enhanced security.

- Customizable hardware and software configurations.

- Greater control over resources.

Advantages:

- **Enhanced Security:** Suitable for handling sensitive data.

- **Regulatory Compliance:** Easier to meet data sovereignty and privacy requirements.

- **Customization:** Tailored to specific organizational needs.

Challenges:

- Higher costs due to dedicated resources.

- Requires in-house expertise for maintenance.

Use Cases:

- Financial institutions requiring strict data security.

- Healthcare organizations managing electronic health records (EHR).

- Government agencies adhering to data sovereignty laws.

---

3. Hybrid Cloud

Definition:
A hybrid cloud integrates public and private clouds, allowing organizations to leverage the benefits of both. This model enables data and applications to move seamlessly between environments.

Key Features:

- Flexibility to run workloads where they perform best.

- Support for both cloud-native and legacy applications.

- Centralized management tools for monitoring and control.

Advantages:

- **Optimized Costs:** Run sensitive workloads on private clouds and use public clouds for scalability.

- **Business Continuity:** Enhanced disaster recovery and backup options.

- **Agility:** Rapid deployment of applications across multiple environments.

Challenges:

- Complexity in integration and management.

- Potential security vulnerabilities during data transfer.

Use Cases:

- Retail businesses balancing customer-facing apps (public cloud) with payment processing systems (private cloud).

- Manufacturing firms using IoT devices connected to edge computing in a hybrid setup.

Key Cloud Service Models: IaaS, PaaS, and SaaS

Cloud services are offered in three primary models, each catering to different levels of user control and responsibility.

1. Infrastructure as a Service (IaaS)

Definition:
IaaS provides virtualized computing resources over the internet, such as servers, storage, and networking. It offers maximum control to users, who are responsible for managing applications, data, and middleware.

Features:

- Pay-as-you-go billing for infrastructure usage.

- Full control over the operating system and installed applications.

Advantages:

- Flexible and scalable.

- Suitable for businesses needing extensive customization.

- Reduces the need for on-premises hardware.

Challenges:

- Users are responsible for managing and securing their systems.

- Requires technical expertise to configure and maintain.

Use Cases:

- Hosting virtual machines and applications.

- Running high-performance computing tasks.

- Disaster recovery and backup solutions.

Examples of IaaS Providers:

- Amazon Web Services (AWS) EC2.

- Microsoft Azure Virtual Machines.

- Google Cloud Compute Engine.

---

2. Platform as a Service (PaaS)

Definition:
PaaS offers a platform for developers to build, test, and deploy applications without worrying about the underlying infrastructure. It includes tools, frameworks, and runtime environments.

Features:

- Pre-configured development environments.

- Integrated tools for application development and deployment.

Advantages:

- Simplifies application development processes.

- Reduces time-to-market for new applications.

- No need to manage hardware or middleware.

Challenges:

- Limited control over underlying infrastructure.

- Dependency on the provider's platform and tools.

Use Cases:

- Developing mobile and web applications.

- Building microservices architectures.

- Automating DevOps workflows.

Examples of PaaS Providers:

- AWS Elastic Beanstalk.

- Google App Engine.

- Microsoft Azure App Service.

---

3. Software as a Service (SaaS)

Definition:
SaaS delivers fully functional applications over the internet. Users access software through web

browsers or APIs, with no need to install or manage the application on their devices.

Features:

- Fully managed by the provider.

- Accessible from any device with internet connectivity.

Advantages:

- Easy to use and deploy.

- Automatic updates and maintenance.

- Predictable subscription-based pricing.

Challenges:

- Limited customization options.

- Dependency on internet connectivity.

Use Cases:

- Customer Relationship Management (CRM) systems.

- Collaboration tools like email and video conferencing.

- Enterprise Resource Planning (ERP) software.

Examples of SaaS Providers:

- Salesforce.

- Google Workspace (Gmail, Google Drive).
- Microsoft Office 365.

Major Cloud Providers and Their Offerings

The cloud computing landscape is dominated by a few key players who provide a wide range of services tailored to diverse business needs.

1. Amazon Web Services (AWS)

Overview:
AWS is the largest cloud provider, offering a comprehensive suite of services. Known for its scalability, reliability, and innovation, AWS serves businesses of all sizes.

Popular Services:

- **EC2 (IaaS):** Virtual servers for scalable computing.
- **S3 (Storage):** Highly durable object storage.
- **Lambda (Serverless):** Event-driven serverless computing.

Use Cases:

- Hosting e-commerce websites.

- Running machine learning workloads.

- Storing and analyzing big data.

2. Microsoft Azure

Overview:
Azure is a leading cloud platform with strong integration capabilities for Microsoft products. It appeals to enterprises with existing Microsoft ecosystems.

Popular Services:

- **Azure Virtual Machines (IaaS):** Scalable compute resources.

- **Azure Functions (PaaS):** Serverless computing.

- **Azure SQL Database (SaaS):** Fully managed relational databases.

Use Cases:

- Migrating on-premises Windows servers.

- Building hybrid cloud solutions.

- Developing AI-powered applications.

3. Google Cloud Platform (GCP)

Overview:
GCP emphasizes data analytics and machine learning capabilities, making it a favorite for research and innovation-driven businesses.

Popular Services:

- **Compute Engine (IaaS):** Virtual machines for high-performance workloads.

- **BigQuery (PaaS):** Serverless data warehouse for analytics.

- **Cloud AI (SaaS):** Pre-built AI models and APIs.

Use Cases:

- Processing and analyzing large datasets.

- Hosting mobile applications.

- Integrating AI-driven solutions into business processes.

Understanding the basics of cloud computing is essential for navigating today's IT landscape. The distinctions between public, private, and hybrid clouds, as well as the benefits of service models like IaaS, PaaS, and SaaS, offer organizations diverse paths to innovation, scalability, and efficiency.

By leveraging offerings from major providers like AWS, Microsoft Azure, and Google Cloud, businesses can build robust, flexible, and secure environments tailored to their unique needs. As we move forward, exploring advanced topics like cloud security, data management, and hybrid cloud integration will further enhance your ability to harness the full potential of cloud computing.

Chapter 4: Why Choose a Hybrid Cloud Strategy?

As organizations navigate the rapidly evolving technology landscape, hybrid cloud strategies have emerged as a compelling solution for balancing the demands of innovation, operational efficiency, and regulatory compliance. Hybrid cloud bridges the gap between traditional on-premises infrastructure and modern cloud computing platforms, empowering businesses with the flexibility to optimize their IT environments.

This chapter explores the key reasons why organizations adopt hybrid cloud strategies, delving into common use cases, strategic advantages, and critical considerations related to cost, scalability, and compliance.

Common Scenarios for Hybrid Cloud Adoption

Hybrid cloud adoption is driven by a variety of scenarios where neither a fully on-premises nor a fully cloud-based solution can meet all organizational needs. These scenarios highlight the flexibility and versatility of the hybrid cloud model.

---

1. Supporting Legacy Applications

Many organizations have critical legacy applications that cannot easily be migrated to the cloud due to compatibility issues, high migration costs, or technical constraints. Hybrid cloud allows these applications to remain on-premises while enabling integration with cloud-based services.

Example Scenario:

- A financial institution maintains its core banking application on-premises but uses a public cloud for running analytics and customer-facing mobile applications.

---

2. Handling Fluctuating Workloads

Organizations with variable workloads benefit from hybrid cloud strategies by using the cloud's scalability during peak periods while relying on on-premises infrastructure for baseline operations.

Example Scenario:

- An e-commerce company uses its on-premises servers for regular operations but scales up to the cloud during high-demand events like Black Friday sales.

3. Ensuring Business Continuity

Hybrid cloud environments enhance disaster recovery and backup strategies by providing redundancy across on-premises and cloud resources.

Example Scenario:

- A healthcare provider stores patient records on-premises for compliance but replicates them to the cloud for disaster recovery purposes.

4. Facilitating Data Sovereignty

Certain industries face stringent regulatory requirements that mandate data be stored within specific geographic regions. Hybrid cloud allows businesses to meet these requirements by keeping sensitive data on-premises while leveraging cloud services for non-sensitive workloads.

Example Scenario:

- A multinational corporation stores sensitive customer data locally while using global cloud services for analytics.

---

5. Enabling Innovation and Experimentation

Hybrid cloud enables organizations to experiment with emerging technologies and cloud-native applications without disrupting their core IT operations.

Example Scenario:

- A manufacturing firm deploys IoT solutions in the cloud to monitor equipment performance while running its ERP system on-premises.

Strategic Advantages for Businesses

Hybrid cloud strategies provide businesses with a competitive edge by addressing unique challenges and unlocking new opportunities. Below are the key strategic advantages.

1. Flexibility and Agility

Hybrid cloud environments allow organizations to run workloads where they perform best—on-premises for critical, latency-sensitive tasks and in the cloud for scalable, dynamic workloads. This flexibility ensures that businesses can adapt quickly to changing demands.

2. Improved Resource Utilization

By combining the strengths of on-premises and cloud infrastructure, hybrid strategies optimize resource utilization. Organizations can reduce waste and improve ROI by aligning workloads with the most cost-effective and efficient resources.

3. Accelerated Innovation

Hybrid cloud empowers businesses to adopt emerging technologies like artificial intelligence (AI), machine learning, and big data analytics without overhauling existing systems. Cloud providers offer cutting-edge tools and platforms that integrate seamlessly with on-premises systems.

4. Enhanced Security and Control

Hybrid cloud offers a balance between the security of on-premises systems and the scalability of the cloud. Businesses retain control over sensitive data while leveraging robust cloud security measures for less critical workloads.

5. Business Continuity and Disaster Recovery

Hybrid cloud environments support robust business continuity strategies. Organizations can replicate data and applications across on-premises and cloud systems, ensuring minimal disruption during outages or disasters.

Cost, Scalability, and Compliance Considerations

While hybrid cloud strategies offer numerous benefits, businesses must carefully evaluate their impact on costs, scalability, and compliance to ensure successful implementation.

1. Cost Considerations

Hybrid cloud strategies can lead to significant cost savings, but they also require careful financial planning to avoid unexpected expenses.

Benefits:

- **Optimized IT Spending:** By running steady workloads on-premises and using the cloud for bursts of demand, businesses can avoid overprovisioning resources.

- **Pay-as-You-Go Pricing:** Cloud services allow businesses to pay only for what they use, reducing capital expenditures.

Challenges:

- **Hidden Costs:** Data transfer fees between on-premises and cloud environments can add up.

- **Infrastructure Maintenance:** On-premises systems still require maintenance, upgrades, and staffing.

Best Practices:

- Conduct a thorough cost analysis to compare on-premises and cloud expenses.

- Use cost-monitoring tools to track and optimize hybrid cloud spending.

2. Scalability Considerations

Scalability is one of the most compelling reasons to adopt a hybrid cloud strategy, enabling businesses to adjust resources in real time.

Benefits:

- **Elasticity:** Cloud services scale automatically to meet demand, eliminating the need for excess on-premises capacity.

- **Global Reach:** Public cloud providers offer access to resources worldwide, ensuring low-latency performance for global operations.

Challenges:

- **Integration Complexity:** Seamless scalability requires robust integration between on-premises and cloud systems.

- **Performance Bottlenecks:** Data transfer between environments can introduce latency and impact application performance.

Best Practices:

- Implement load-balancing solutions to distribute workloads effectively.

- Optimize data transfer paths to reduce latency and maximize performance.

3. Compliance Considerations

Hybrid cloud strategies can simplify compliance with regulatory requirements, but they also introduce complexities that must be managed carefully.

Benefits:

- **Data Sovereignty:** Businesses can store sensitive data on-premises to meet legal requirements while using the cloud for other operations.

- **Auditing and Reporting:** Cloud providers offer compliance tools that help businesses monitor and report adherence to regulations.

Challenges:

- **Data Privacy:** Ensuring consistent privacy practices across on-premises and cloud systems is critical.

- **Regulatory Complexity:** Organizations operating in multiple regions must navigate different compliance standards.

Best Practices:

- Work with legal and compliance teams to develop policies for hybrid environments.

- Use encryption and identity management tools to secure data across systems.

Real-World Examples of Hybrid Cloud Success

To illustrate the benefits of hybrid cloud strategies, consider the following examples:

1. **Retail Industry:**
   A retail chain uses hybrid cloud to integrate its point-of-sale (POS) systems with cloud-based analytics. Real-time sales data is processed in the cloud to predict inventory needs, while sensitive payment data remains on-premises for security.

2. **Healthcare Sector:**
   A hospital network stores patient records on-premises to comply with HIPAA regulations while using the cloud to provide telemedicine services and run AI diagnostics.

3. **Financial Services:**
   A bank deploys a hybrid cloud to maintain on-premises control over transaction data while utilizing cloud-based applications for

customer relationship management (CRM) and fraud detection.

The hybrid cloud offers a transformative approach to IT infrastructure, empowering businesses to balance the advantages of on-premises systems with the scalability and innovation of the cloud. By addressing common scenarios, leveraging strategic advantages, and carefully managing costs, scalability, and compliance, organizations can unlock the full potential of this versatile model.

As technology continues to evolve, hybrid cloud strategies will remain a cornerstone of digital transformation, enabling businesses to adapt, innovate, and thrive in an increasingly dynamic world. In the next chapter, we will explore the architecture of hybrid cloud solutions and delve into best practices for seamless integration.

Chapter 5: Planning a Hybrid Cloud Implementation

Implementing a hybrid cloud strategy requires meticulous planning, a clear understanding of current infrastructure, and a well-defined roadmap to ensure success. This chapter provides a step-by-step guide to assessing existing systems, setting achievable goals, defining key performance indicators (KPIs), and creating a migration roadmap for seamless hybrid cloud integration.

Assessing Existing Infrastructure and Workloads

Before embarking on a hybrid cloud implementation, organizations must conduct a thorough assessment of their existing IT infrastructure and workloads. This foundational step ensures the hybrid cloud solution is aligned with current capabilities and future needs.

1. Inventory Existing Infrastructure

A comprehensive inventory of existing resources provides a clear picture of the organization's IT landscape. Key elements to assess include:

- **Servers:** Physical and virtual servers, their configurations, and performance.

- **Storage Systems:** Types of storage (NAS, SAN, DAS), capacity, and usage patterns.

- **Networking:** Network topology, bandwidth, and latency metrics.

- **Applications:** Business-critical applications, their dependencies, and current hosting environments.

- **Security Infrastructure:** Firewalls, intrusion detection systems, and encryption protocols.

Actionable Steps:

- Use automated tools to generate a detailed inventory report.

- Identify outdated or underutilized resources that may impact cloud migration.

2. Classify Workloads

Not all workloads are suitable for the cloud, and some may perform better on-premises. Classifying workloads helps determine the best placement for each.

Categories of Workloads:

- **Static Workloads:** Consistent demand, suitable for on-premises systems.

- **Dynamic Workloads:** Fluctuating demand, ideal for cloud environments.

- **Latency-Sensitive Workloads:** Require low-latency, often kept on-premises.

- **Compliance-Critical Workloads:** Must adhere to strict regulations, favoring on-premises or private clouds.

Actionable Steps:

- Evaluate workload performance metrics (CPU, memory, storage, and network usage).

- Identify dependencies and interactions between workloads to prevent disruptions during migration.

3. Evaluate Current Challenges and Pain Points

Understanding existing challenges can inform the design of the hybrid cloud strategy. Common issues include:

- Resource limitations leading to performance bottlenecks.

- High operational costs for maintaining legacy systems.

- Lack of scalability to meet business growth.

Actionable Steps:

- Conduct stakeholder interviews to identify recurring IT challenges.

- Map current inefficiencies to potential solutions offered by hybrid cloud models.

Setting Goals and KPIs for Hybrid Cloud Integration

Establishing clear goals and measurable KPIs ensures the hybrid cloud implementation aligns with organizational objectives. Goals provide direction, while KPIs help track progress and measure success.

1. Define Strategic Objectives

The goals of a hybrid cloud implementation should reflect the organization's broader business strategy. Examples include:

- **Enhancing Scalability:** Ensure IT systems can handle rapid growth or seasonal demand spikes.

- **Optimizing Costs:** Reduce capital expenditures by leveraging cloud resources.

- **Improving Agility:** Enable faster development, testing, and deployment of applications.

- **Strengthening Security:** Protect sensitive data while meeting compliance requirements.

Actionable Steps:

- Align hybrid cloud goals with key business priorities, such as customer satisfaction or market expansion.

- Engage stakeholders from different departments to ensure goals are inclusive and realistic.

2. Establish KPIs

Key Performance Indicators (KPIs) provide measurable metrics to evaluate the success of the hybrid cloud strategy. Common KPIs include:

- **Cost Metrics:** Reduction in capital expenditures (CapEx) and operational expenditures (OpEx).

- **Performance Metrics:** Improved application response times and reduced latency.

- **Scalability Metrics:** Time taken to provision new resources or scale workloads.

- **Security Metrics:** Number of security incidents, compliance audit success rates.

- **User Satisfaction Metrics:** Employee and customer satisfaction with IT services.

Actionable Steps:

- Use baseline metrics from current infrastructure to set realistic targets.

- Regularly review and refine KPIs to reflect evolving business needs.

Creating a Migration Roadmap

A migration roadmap outlines the step-by-step process for transitioning to a hybrid cloud environment. It serves as a blueprint to guide the implementation, minimizing risks and disruptions.

---

1. Develop a Phased Approach

Hybrid cloud migration is a complex process that benefits from being broken into manageable phases.

Phases of Migration:

1. **Preparation Phase:**
   - Conduct infrastructure assessments.
   - Define goals and KPIs.
   - Secure stakeholder buy-in and allocate resources.

2. **Pilot Phase:**
   - Identify a small, non-critical workload to migrate as a test case.
   - Validate the hybrid cloud setup, including integration, performance, and security.

3. **Execution Phase:**

   o Gradually migrate workloads based on priority and complexity.

   o Monitor performance and adjust configurations as needed.

4. **Optimization Phase:**

   o Analyze post-migration performance metrics.

   o Optimize resource allocation and refine processes.

Actionable Steps:

- Create a detailed timeline for each phase.
- Assign responsibilities to team members and ensure accountability.

---

2. Select Hybrid Cloud Tools and Platforms

The success of a hybrid cloud strategy depends on choosing the right tools and platforms for integration, management, and security.

Key Tools:

- **Integration Platforms:** Enable seamless communication between on-premises and cloud environments (e.g., APIs, middleware).

- **Management Tools:** Provide centralized control and monitoring of hybrid systems.

- **Security Solutions:** Ensure data encryption, identity management, and threat detection across environments.

Actionable Steps:

- Evaluate tools based on compatibility with existing infrastructure.

- Prioritize platforms that align with organizational goals and technical expertise.

---

3. Address Security and Compliance

Security is a top priority in hybrid cloud implementations, especially when sensitive data is involved.

Key Considerations:

- **Data Encryption:** Encrypt data in transit and at rest across all environments.

- **Identity and Access Management (IAM):** Implement role-based access control and multi-factor authentication.

- **Compliance Audits:** Ensure the hybrid cloud setup adheres to industry regulations (e.g., GDPR, HIPAA).

Actionable Steps:

- Develop a security framework tailored to the hybrid cloud environment.

- Conduct regular security assessments and audits.

4. Train and Upskill Teams

Hybrid cloud implementations require skilled personnel capable of managing both on-premises and cloud systems.

Key Training Areas:

- Cloud platform operation (AWS, Azure, Google Cloud).

- Hybrid cloud management and troubleshooting.

- Best practices for data security and compliance.

Actionable Steps:

- Offer training programs and certifications for IT staff.

- Foster collaboration between on-premises and cloud teams to ensure seamless operations.

5. Monitor and Optimize

The hybrid cloud journey doesn't end with migration. Continuous monitoring and optimization are crucial for long-term success.

Key Areas of Focus:

- **Performance Monitoring:** Track resource utilization, response times, and workload distribution.

- **Cost Optimization:** Identify and eliminate unnecessary expenditures.

- **Scalability Testing:** Periodically test the ability to handle increased workloads.

Actionable Steps:

- Use monitoring tools to generate real-time insights.

- Establish a feedback loop to address issues promptly and improve processes.

Case Study: Hybrid Cloud Migration in Action

Scenario:
A mid-sized retail chain wanted to modernize its IT infrastructure to improve customer experiences and operational efficiency.

Challenges:

- Legacy systems were unable to handle growing e-commerce traffic.

- Data privacy regulations required sensitive customer data to remain on-premises.

Hybrid Cloud Implementation:

1. **Assessment:** The company inventoried its infrastructure and identified critical workloads for migration.

2. **Goal Setting:** Objectives included reducing downtime, improving scalability, and maintaining compliance.

3. **Pilot Migration:** The e-commerce application's backend was migrated to a public cloud, while customer data remained on-premises.

4. **Optimization:** Performance metrics were monitored, and the system was fine-tuned to handle peak traffic.

Outcome:
The hybrid cloud strategy reduced operational costs by 25%, improved website performance, and ensured compliance with data regulations.

Planning a hybrid cloud implementation is a complex but rewarding process that requires a strategic approach, careful assessment, and detailed planning. By understanding existing infrastructure, setting clear goals and KPIs, and creating a comprehensive migration roadmap, organizations can unlock the full potential of hybrid cloud environments.

In the next chapter, we will explore hybrid cloud architecture, providing insights into designing systems that maximize efficiency and reliability.

Chapter 6: Architecture of Hybrid Cloud Solutions

A well-designed architecture is the foundation of any successful hybrid cloud strategy. It enables seamless communication between on-premises and cloud environments, ensures scalability and security, and provides the flexibility needed to meet business objectives. This chapter explores the key architectural components of hybrid cloud solutions, design patterns for integration, and the considerations for leveraging multi-cloud versus hybrid cloud setups.

Key Architectural Components: APIs, Gateways, and Connectors

Hybrid cloud solutions rely on a variety of components to ensure smooth integration and interoperability between different environments. Among these, APIs, gateways, and connectors play critical roles.

1. Application Programming Interfaces (APIs)

Definition:
APIs act as the communication bridges between different systems, allowing applications in on-premises and cloud environments to exchange data and functionality seamlessly.

Roles of APIs in Hybrid Cloud:

- **Interoperability:** APIs ensure that on-premises applications can interact with cloud-based services.

- **Automation:** APIs facilitate automated workflows, enabling faster deployment and scaling of applications.

- **Extensibility:** APIs allow developers to extend the functionality of applications by integrating external services.

Examples of Hybrid Cloud APIs:

- REST APIs for interacting with cloud storage or databases.

- Cloud provider APIs like AWS SDK, Azure APIs, and Google Cloud APIs for managing resources programmatically.

Best Practices:

- Use standard API formats (e.g., REST, GraphQL) to ensure compatibility.

- Implement API versioning to maintain backward compatibility during updates.

- Secure APIs with authentication protocols such as OAuth or API keys.

2. Gateways

Definition:
Gateways serve as intermediaries that manage, monitor, and secure communication between on-premises systems and cloud environments.

Roles of Gateways in Hybrid Cloud:

- **Traffic Management:** Gateways optimize the flow of data between environments, reducing latency and ensuring efficient use of bandwidth.

- **Security Enforcement:** Gateways provide encryption, authentication, and firewalls to protect data in transit.

- **Protocol Translation:** Gateways translate communication protocols to enable compatibility between different systems.

Examples of Gateways:

- API Gateways like AWS API Gateway and Azure API Management.

- Network Gateways for connecting on-premises networks with cloud environments using VPNs or Direct Connect.

Best Practices:

- Deploy gateways close to the systems they serve to minimize latency.

- Monitor gateway performance to identify and resolve bottlenecks.

---

3. Connectors

Definition:
Connectors are pre-built tools or frameworks that enable integration between specific systems or services, simplifying the process of connecting diverse applications.

Roles of Connectors in Hybrid Cloud:

- **Pre-Built Integration:** Connectors reduce the time and complexity of connecting systems.

- **Data Synchronization:** They ensure consistent data exchange between on-premises and cloud environments.

- **Vendor-Specific Features:** Connectors often come optimized for specific platforms, leveraging advanced functionalities.

Examples of Connectors:

- Cloud storage connectors for syncing on-premises data with cloud storage services.

- Application-specific connectors, such as Salesforce Connect for hybrid CRM integration.

Best Practices:

- Choose connectors compatible with existing applications and workflows.

- Regularly update connectors to ensure security and performance.

Design Patterns for Seamless Integration

Hybrid cloud architecture requires thoughtful design patterns to ensure that on-premises and cloud systems operate as a cohesive unit. Below are some common design patterns that enable seamless integration.

---

1. Hub-and-Spoke Architecture

Overview:
In this pattern, a central hub coordinates communication between various systems and environments. The hub acts as a middleware layer that processes requests, applies policies, and routes data to the appropriate destination.

Benefits:

- Simplifies management by centralizing control.

- Enhances security with a single point for applying policies.

- Supports scalability by adding spokes as needed.

Use Case:
A retail business using a central hub to synchronize inventory data across on-premises systems and multiple cloud platforms.

---

2. Data Fabric Architecture

Overview:
Data fabric provides a unified layer for managing, accessing, and securing data across hybrid environments. It decouples data storage from compute resources, enabling seamless data integration.

Benefits:

- Facilitates consistent data access across environments.

- Simplifies compliance by centralizing data governance.

- Enhances performance by optimizing data placement.

Use Case:
A healthcare organization integrating patient records stored on-premises with cloud-based analytics platforms.

3. Event-Driven Architecture

Overview:
This pattern uses events as triggers for communication and processing. It ensures real-time updates and decouples systems for greater flexibility.

Benefits:

- Supports real-time data processing and responsiveness.

- Reduces system coupling, enabling independent updates.

- Improves scalability by distributing workloads dynamically.

Use Case:
An IoT system that triggers cloud-based analytics whenever on-premises sensors detect anomalies.

---

4. Microservices Architecture

Overview:
Applications are broken into smaller, independent services that can run in different environments. These microservices communicate through APIs, making them ideal for hybrid cloud deployments.

Benefits:

- Enhances flexibility and scalability.

- Simplifies updates by isolating changes to individual services.

- Supports diverse environments by running microservices where they perform best.

Use Case:
A financial institution developing microservices for payment processing, fraud detection, and reporting across hybrid environments.

Leveraging Multi-Cloud vs. Hybrid Cloud Setups

Although hybrid cloud and multi-cloud setups share similarities, they serve different purposes and offer distinct benefits.

Hybrid Cloud

Definition:
Hybrid cloud integrates on-premises infrastructure with one or more cloud platforms, creating a unified environment.

Key Characteristics:

- Focused on bridging on-premises and cloud systems.

- Ideal for organizations with legacy systems or strict compliance requirements.

- Ensures a consistent management experience across environments.

Benefits:

- Greater control over sensitive data.

- Tailored workload distribution for optimal performance.

- Robust disaster recovery through integrated backup solutions.

Challenges:

- Complex integration and configuration requirements.

- Potential latency issues during data transfer.

Use Case:
A manufacturing firm using on-premises systems for production control and cloud services for analytics.

Multi-Cloud

Definition:
Multi-cloud involves using multiple cloud providers to meet diverse business needs. Unlike hybrid cloud, it does not necessarily involve on-premises systems.

Key Characteristics:

- Focused on leveraging multiple public or private cloud platforms.

- Provides flexibility to choose the best provider for specific workloads.

- Minimizes vendor lock-in by distributing resources across providers.

Benefits:

- Access to a broader range of tools and services.

- Increased redundancy and resilience.

- Competitive pricing by negotiating with multiple providers.

Challenges:

- Requires expertise to manage diverse cloud platforms.

- Complex interoperability and data migration issues.

Use Case:
A global enterprise using AWS for compute resources, Google Cloud for data analytics, and Azure for AI capabilities.

Key Considerations for Hybrid and Multi-Cloud Setups

1. **Integration Complexity:**

   - Ensure seamless communication between environments using APIs, gateways, and connectors.

   - Standardize processes to reduce operational complexity.

2. **Security and Compliance:**

   - Implement unified security policies across all environments.

   - Use tools that support multi-cloud and hybrid cloud governance.

3. **Cost Management:**

   - Monitor expenses with cloud cost optimization tools.

   - Analyze workload placement to avoid unnecessary expenditures.

4. **Performance Optimization:**

   - Use edge computing for latency-sensitive applications.

   - Monitor performance metrics to identify and address bottlenecks.

The architecture of hybrid cloud solutions is critical to unlocking their full potential. By leveraging components like APIs, gateways, and connectors, adopting proven design patterns, and understanding the nuances of multi-cloud and hybrid cloud setups, organizations can build flexible, scalable, and secure IT environments.

Chapter 7: Networking for Hybrid Cloud Environments

Networking is the backbone of hybrid cloud environments, facilitating secure and efficient communication between on-premises infrastructure, cloud platforms, and users. Without robust networking, the hybrid cloud cannot deliver the reliability, performance, and security required for modern IT workloads. This chapter explores the essential components of networking in hybrid cloud environments, with a focus on configuring secure and reliable connectivity, virtual private networks (VPNs) and direct connect options, and best practices for network management and monitoring.

Configuring Secure and Reliable Connectivity

In a hybrid cloud setup, secure and reliable connectivity ensures seamless data exchange between on-premises systems and cloud platforms while safeguarding sensitive information from unauthorized access.

1. Core Principles of Hybrid Cloud Networking

a. Security
Security is paramount in hybrid cloud environments, where data frequently traverses public and private networks. Organizations must protect data in transit and at rest by implementing encryption, firewalls, and access controls.

b. Reliability
Hybrid cloud networking requires consistent and uninterrupted connectivity to prevent disruptions to critical applications and services.

c. Scalability
As workloads grow, the network must scale to accommodate increased data traffic without compromising performance.

d. Low Latency
For real-time applications, such as video conferencing or IoT devices, minimizing latency is critical to ensuring a smooth user experience.

2. Key Connectivity Models

Hybrid cloud networks typically use one or more of the following connectivity models:

a. Internet-Based Connectivity
Organizations can connect their on-premises infrastructure to the cloud over the public internet using secure protocols like HTTPS or VPNs. While cost-effective, this option may introduce latency and potential security risks.

b. Dedicated Connectivity
Dedicated connectivity options, such as direct connections or leased lines, offer private, high-speed links between environments, ensuring superior performance and security.

c. Hybrid WAN
A hybrid wide-area network (WAN) combines public internet and private connections to provide a balance between cost and performance.

3. Tools for Configuring Secure Connectivity

a. Encryption Protocols
Encrypt data using protocols like IPsec, SSL/TLS, or HTTPS to ensure secure communication.

b. Firewalls
Deploy firewalls at network boundaries to filter traffic and block unauthorized access.

c. Identity and Access Management (IAM)
Use IAM solutions to enforce authentication and authorization policies for accessing network resources.

d. Network Segmentation
Divide the network into isolated segments to contain potential security breaches and improve traffic management.

Virtual Private Networks (VPNs) and Direct Connect Options

VPNs and direct connect solutions are fundamental to hybrid cloud networking, providing secure and efficient connections between on-premises and cloud environments.

---

1. Virtual Private Networks (VPNs)

Definition:
A VPN creates an encrypted tunnel over the internet, enabling secure communication between on-premises systems and cloud resources.

Advantages of VPNs:

- **Cost-Effective:** VPNs leverage the public internet, eliminating the need for dedicated infrastructure.

- **Ease of Deployment:** VPNs are straightforward to configure and can be implemented quickly.

- **Security:** VPNs encrypt data in transit, protecting it from interception.

Types of VPNs:

- **Site-to-Site VPNs:** Connect entire networks, making them ideal for linking data centers and cloud environments.

- **Client-to-Site VPNs:** Allow individual devices to securely access the hybrid cloud.

Challenges:

- VPNs can introduce latency due to encryption overhead and internet traffic.

- Bandwidth limitations may affect performance during peak usage.

2. Direct Connect Options

Definition:
Direct connect solutions provide dedicated, private connections between on-premises infrastructure and cloud platforms, bypassing the public internet.

Advantages of Direct Connect:

- **High Performance:** Direct connections offer consistent, low-latency communication.

- **Enhanced Security:** Private links reduce exposure to internet-based threats.

- **Scalability:** Direct connect solutions can handle large volumes of data traffic.

Examples of Direct Connect Services:

- **AWS Direct Connect:** Provides a dedicated connection to AWS services.

- **Azure ExpressRoute:** Offers private connections to Microsoft Azure.

- **Google Cloud Interconnect:** Enables private communication with Google Cloud.

Challenges:

- Direct connect options involve higher costs compared to VPNs.

- Deployment requires collaboration with service providers, which can extend timelines.

---

3. Choosing Between VPNs and Direct Connect

Factors to Consider:

- **Budget:** VPNs are more cost-effective, while direct connect solutions require higher upfront investment.

- **Performance Needs:** Direct connect is better suited for latency-sensitive or high-bandwidth applications.

- **Security Requirements:** Organizations with stringent security policies may prefer direct connect.

Best Practices for Network Management and Monitoring

Effective network management and monitoring are essential for ensuring the performance, security, and reliability of hybrid cloud environments.

---

1. Proactive Network Management

a. Centralized Management
Use centralized tools to manage hybrid networks across on-premises and cloud environments. These tools provide visibility into traffic, performance, and security.

b. Automation
Leverage automation for tasks like configuration updates, traffic routing, and policy enforcement to reduce manual errors and improve efficiency.

c. Scalability Planning
Design networks to accommodate growth, ensuring sufficient bandwidth and capacity for future demands.

d. Redundancy and Failover
Implement redundant connections and failover mechanisms to maintain connectivity during outages or hardware failures.

2. Comprehensive Network Monitoring

a. Monitoring Tools
Deploy network monitoring solutions to track key performance metrics, such as latency, packet loss, and throughput.

Examples of Monitoring Tools:

- **SolarWinds Network Performance Monitor:** Offers real-time network visibility and analytics.

- **AWS CloudWatch:** Provides monitoring for AWS-based hybrid cloud environments.

- **Nagios:** Monitors on-premises and hybrid network health.

b. Real-Time Alerts
Set up alerts for anomalies, such as unusual traffic patterns or potential security breaches, to enable swift response.

c. End-to-End Visibility
Ensure monitoring covers the entire hybrid cloud network, including on-premises systems, cloud platforms, and data transfer points.

---

3. Security Best Practices

a. Zero Trust Architecture
Adopt a zero-trust model, where no entity is trusted by default, even within the network. Implement multi-factor authentication (MFA) and continuous verification.

b. Network Segmentation
Isolate sensitive workloads and restrict access to specific segments of the network.

c. Regular Audits
Conduct routine security audits to identify vulnerabilities and ensure compliance with regulations.

d. Threat Detection and Response
Deploy intrusion detection systems (IDS) and intrusion prevention systems (IPS) to identify and mitigate threats.

Case Study: Hybrid Cloud Networking in Action

Scenario:
A global logistics company faced challenges managing its growing hybrid cloud environment, with latency issues affecting real-time package tracking and data security concerns during transfers.

Solution:

1. **VPN Deployment:** Site-to-site VPNs were implemented to secure communication between regional offices and the cloud.

2. **Direct Connect for Performance:** AWS Direct Connect was used to link critical data centers with AWS, ensuring low-latency access for package tracking applications.

3. **Network Monitoring:** SolarWinds was deployed for centralized monitoring, enabling the IT team to track performance and detect anomalies.

4. **Redundancy:** Redundant connections were established to ensure uninterrupted operations during outages.

Outcome:
The company achieved a 30% improvement in application performance, reduced downtime, and enhanced data security across its hybrid cloud network.

Networking is the backbone of hybrid cloud environments, enabling secure and efficient communication between on-premises and cloud systems. By carefully configuring connectivity, selecting the right solutions like VPNs or direct connect, and adhering to best practices for network management and monitoring, organizations can build robust networks that meet their operational needs.

In the next chapter, we will explore data management in hybrid cloud environments, focusing on synchronization, governance, and compliance strategies to ensure secure and efficient operations.

Chapter 8: Data Management in a Hybrid Cloud

Data management is a cornerstone of hybrid cloud strategies, enabling organizations to synchronize, secure, and govern data across on-premises and cloud environments. Effectively managing data ensures seamless operations, regulatory compliance, and robust disaster recovery capabilities. This chapter delves into the critical aspects of data management in a hybrid cloud, including synchronizing and migrating data, addressing governance and compliance challenges, and implementing strategies for backup, disaster recovery, and data replication.

Synchronizing and Migrating Data Between Environments

Hybrid cloud architectures depend on efficient data synchronization and migration to ensure that on-premises and cloud environments function cohesively. This requires careful planning and the use of appropriate tools to avoid data loss, minimize downtime, and ensure compatibility.

---

1. Data Synchronization

Definition:
Data synchronization involves ensuring that data is consistent and up to date across multiple environments. This is particularly critical in hybrid cloud setups where applications may access data stored in different locations.

Key Considerations for Synchronization:

- **Latency:** Real-time or near-real-time synchronization is essential for time-sensitive applications.

- **Data Consistency:** Maintaining data integrity across environments prevents errors and inconsistencies.

- **Conflict Resolution:** Managing updates from multiple sources requires conflict resolution policies.

Tools for Data Synchronization:

- **AWS DataSync:** Automates moving and synchronizing data between on-premises storage and AWS.

- **Azure Data Factory:** Facilitates data integration and transformation across hybrid environments.

- **Google Cloud Transfer Service:** Enables seamless data transfers and synchronization.

---

2. Data Migration

Definition:
Data migration involves transferring data from on-premises systems to the cloud or between different cloud platforms as part of a hybrid cloud strategy.

Types of Data Migration:

- **Lift-and-Shift Migration:** Moves data as-is without modifications.

- **Re-Platforming:** Adapts data to leverage cloud-native features.

- **Data Transformation:** Involves reformatting or restructuring data to suit new environments.

Steps for a Successful Migration:

1. **Assessment:** Inventory existing data, evaluate dependencies, and identify critical workloads.

2. **Planning:** Define objectives, select migration tools, and determine a timeline.

3. **Execution:** Perform migrations in stages, prioritizing less critical data before handling mission-critical workloads.

4. **Validation:** Test migrated data for integrity, performance, and accessibility.

Challenges in Data Migration:

- **Downtime:** Migrations can disrupt operations if not carefully managed.

- **Data Loss:** Ensuring no data is lost during migration requires meticulous validation.

- **Performance Impact:** Large-scale migrations can strain network resources.

Best Practices:

- Use migration tools that support incremental data transfers to minimize downtime.

- Encrypt data in transit to ensure security.

- Conduct a pilot migration to identify and address potential issues.

Data Governance, Compliance, and Sovereignty Issues

Hybrid cloud environments introduce unique challenges in data governance, compliance, and sovereignty due to the distributed nature of data storage and processing.

---

1. Data Governance

Definition:
Data governance involves establishing policies, procedures, and standards for managing data to ensure its accuracy, security, and usability.

Key Aspects of Data Governance:

- **Data Quality:** Ensuring data is accurate, complete, and consistent.

- **Access Control:** Implementing policies for who can access, modify, or share data.

- **Auditing:** Tracking data access and modifications for accountability.

Governance Tools:

- **Microsoft Purview:** Provides data discovery, classification, and governance capabilities.

- **AWS Lake Formation:** Simplifies building secure data lakes with governance policies.

- **Collibra:** A platform for data governance and cataloging.

Best Practices:

- Establish a data governance framework aligned with business objectives.

- Define roles and responsibilities for data ownership and stewardship.

- Regularly review and update governance policies to reflect evolving requirements.

---

2. Compliance

Definition:
Compliance refers to adhering to legal and regulatory requirements for data storage, processing, and access. Non-compliance can result in fines, legal actions, and reputational damage.

Common Regulations:

- **GDPR (General Data Protection Regulation):** Governs data privacy in the European Union.

- **HIPAA (Health Insurance Portability and Accountability Act):** Protects healthcare data in the U.S.

- **CCPA (California Consumer Privacy Act):** Regulates data privacy for California residents.

Compliance Strategies for Hybrid Cloud:

- Store sensitive data in environments that meet specific regulatory requirements.

- Use encryption to protect data at rest and in transit.

- Implement logging and auditing to maintain an audit trail of data access and usage.

---

3. Data Sovereignty

Definition:
Data sovereignty refers to the principle that data is subject to the laws and regulations of the country where it is stored. Hybrid cloud environments often involve cross-border data storage, raising sovereignty concerns.

Challenges:

- Ensuring compliance with regional regulations for data stored in different jurisdictions.

- Navigating conflicting laws when data spans multiple countries.

Best Practices:

- Work with cloud providers that offer region-specific storage options.

- Use data localization tools to restrict sensitive data to specific geographic regions.

- Consult legal and compliance teams to address jurisdictional complexities.

Backup, Disaster Recovery, and Data Replication Strategies

In hybrid cloud environments, robust backup, disaster recovery (DR), and replication strategies are critical to ensure data availability, business continuity, and resilience against disruptions.

---

1. Backup Strategies

Definition:
Backups involve creating copies of data to restore it in case of accidental deletion, corruption, or system failures.

Hybrid Cloud Backup Options:

- **On-Premises Backup:** Storing backups locally for quick access and recovery.

- **Cloud Backup:** Using cloud storage to replicate and secure backups.

- **Hybrid Backup:** Combining on-premises and cloud backups for redundancy.

Best Practices:

- Follow the 3-2-1 Backup Rule: Keep three copies of data, stored on two different media types, with one copy off-site.

- Use incremental backups to reduce storage requirements.

- Test backup recovery processes regularly to ensure reliability.

2. Disaster Recovery (DR)

Definition:
Disaster recovery focuses on restoring IT systems and data following a disruption, such as natural disasters, cyberattacks, or hardware failures.

Hybrid Cloud DR Solutions:

- **Cloud DR Services:** Leverage cloud platforms for rapid failover and recovery.

- **Replication-Based DR:** Maintain synchronized copies of critical systems in the cloud.

- **Cold, Warm, and Hot Sites:** Deploy varying levels of standby environments based on recovery time objectives (RTOs).

Best Practices:

- Develop a DR plan that outlines recovery priorities, timelines, and responsibilities.

- Conduct regular DR drills to identify gaps and improve readiness.

- Monitor RTOs and recovery point objectives (RPOs) to meet business requirements.

3. Data Replication

Definition:
Data replication involves creating real-time or near-real-time copies of data across multiple environments to ensure availability and fault tolerance.

Types of Replication:

- **Synchronous Replication:** Data is replicated in real-time, ensuring consistency but requiring low-latency networks.

- **Asynchronous Replication:** Data is replicated with a delay, reducing bandwidth requirements but introducing potential inconsistencies.

Use Cases:

- **High Availability:** Replicate databases across on-premises and cloud systems for uninterrupted service.

- **Geographic Redundancy:** Distribute data across regions to ensure accessibility in case of regional outages.

Best Practices:

- Use tools like AWS Database Migration Service, Azure Site Recovery, or Google Cloud BigQuery for efficient replication.

- Monitor replication processes to identify and resolve bottlenecks.

- Balance consistency and performance requirements when choosing replication methods.

Case Study: Hybrid Cloud Data Management Success

Scenario:
A multinational retail chain faced challenges managing customer data across on-premises systems and multiple cloud platforms while ensuring compliance with GDPR and ensuring disaster recovery capabilities.

Solution:

1. **Data Synchronization:** The organization implemented Azure Data Factory to synchronize customer data across on-premises systems and the cloud.

2. **Compliance:** Sensitive customer information was stored in GDPR-compliant Azure regions, while less sensitive data was processed globally.

3. **Disaster Recovery:** AWS Elastic Disaster Recovery was deployed to replicate critical applications and databases to the cloud for rapid recovery.

4. **Replication:** Asynchronous replication ensured that data from retail locations was updated in near-real-time to centralized systems.

Outcome:
The company achieved 99.99% data availability, reduced downtime by 80%, and ensured full compliance with GDPR regulations.

Data management in hybrid cloud environments is a multifaceted challenge that requires meticulous planning, robust governance, and advanced technologies. By synchronizing and migrating data efficiently, addressing governance and compliance issues, and implementing comprehensive backup, disaster recovery, and replication strategies, organizations can ensure their hybrid cloud deployments are resilient, secure, and future-ready.

In the next chapter, we will explore security strategies for hybrid cloud environments, focusing on protecting data, applications, and networks against modern threats.

Chapter 9: Security in Hybrid Cloud Solutions

Hybrid cloud solutions offer unparalleled flexibility, scalability, and efficiency, but they also introduce unique security challenges. Protecting sensitive data, applications, and infrastructure across on-premises and cloud environments is critical to ensuring business continuity and trust. This chapter explores how to identify vulnerabilities, implement robust access control and identity management, and leverage encryption and monitoring tools to secure hybrid cloud environments effectively.

Identifying Potential Vulnerabilities

A hybrid cloud environment's distributed nature introduces vulnerabilities that must be proactively identified and addressed to ensure comprehensive security.

1. Data in Transit and at Rest

Potential Vulnerabilities:

- **Data in Transit:** Sensitive data moving between on-premises systems and cloud platforms can be intercepted if not properly secured.

- **Data at Rest:** Storing data in multiple environments increases the risk of unauthorized access or breaches.

Examples:

- Unencrypted data transfers.

- Weak storage configurations in cloud environments.

Mitigation Strategies:

- Use encryption protocols such as SSL/TLS for data in transit.

- Implement encryption standards like AES-256 for data at rest.

- Regularly audit storage configurations for vulnerabilities.

2. Misconfigured Access Controls

Potential Vulnerabilities:

- Excessive or insufficient access permissions can expose sensitive data to unauthorized users or hinder operations.

Examples:

- Open access to cloud storage buckets.

- Weak or outdated password policies.

Mitigation Strategies:

- Implement the principle of least privilege (PoLP) to restrict access based on roles.

- Use role-based access control (RBAC) for granular permissions management.

- Regularly review and update access policies.

---

3. Network Vulnerabilities

Potential Vulnerabilities:

- Hybrid cloud networks often rely on public internet connections, exposing them to risks such as man-in-the-middle attacks, DDoS attacks, and unauthorized access.

Examples:

- Unsecured API endpoints.

- Insufficient firewall protections.

Mitigation Strategies:

- Use virtual private networks (VPNs) or dedicated connections like AWS Direct Connect.

- Deploy intrusion detection and prevention systems (IDS/IPS).

- Regularly patch and update network infrastructure.

---

4. Compliance Gaps

Potential Vulnerabilities:

- Operating across multiple jurisdictions introduces complexities in meeting regulatory requirements, such as GDPR, HIPAA, and CCPA.

Examples:

- Data stored in non-compliant regions.

- Inadequate audit trails for sensitive data.

Mitigation Strategies:

- Implement tools to track and manage data sovereignty.

- Use logging and auditing solutions to monitor compliance.

Implementing Robust Access Control and Identity Management

Access control and identity management are vital for protecting hybrid cloud environments from unauthorized access and ensuring accountability.

1. Access Control

a. Principles of Access Control

- **Principle of Least Privilege (PoLP):** Limit access to only what is necessary for users to perform their roles.

- **Separation of Duties:** Divide responsibilities among multiple users to prevent misuse.

b. Role-Based Access Control (RBAC)

- Assign roles to users with predefined permissions for specific tasks.

- Example: A database administrator can access and modify databases, but cannot manage application code.

c. Attribute-Based Access Control (ABAC)

- Implement fine-grained policies based on user attributes, such as location, device type, or time of access.

Best Practices for Access Control:

- Regularly review and revoke unused or outdated permissions.

- Implement time-limited access for temporary tasks.

- Use conditional access policies to enforce rules, such as blocking access from unknown locations.

---

2. Identity and Access Management (IAM)

a. Centralized IAM Solutions

- Use IAM platforms like AWS IAM, Azure Active Directory, or Google Cloud Identity to manage user identities across environments.

b. Multi-Factor Authentication (MFA)

- Require multiple forms of verification, such as passwords and biometric authentication, to strengthen security.

c. Single Sign-On (SSO)

- Implement SSO to allow users to access multiple systems with one set of credentials, improving security and user convenience.

d. Privileged Access Management (PAM)

- Secure accounts with elevated privileges by enforcing stricter access policies, monitoring their activities, and implementing session recording.

---

3. Securing APIs

APIs are critical for communication in hybrid cloud environments, but they also represent a significant attack vector.

Best Practices:

- Use API gateways to manage and secure APIs.

- Require API authentication using OAuth 2.0 or API keys.

- Regularly test APIs for vulnerabilities, such as injection attacks or improper data handling.

Encryption and Monitoring Tools for Hybrid Setups

Encryption and monitoring are essential for safeguarding data and detecting threats in hybrid cloud environments.

1. Encryption

a. Importance of Encryption

- Encryption ensures that data remains unreadable to unauthorized users, even if intercepted or accessed.

b. Types of Encryption

- **Data at Rest Encryption:** Protects stored data using encryption algorithms like AES-256.

- **Data in Transit Encryption:** Secures data as it moves between systems using protocols like SSL/TLS or HTTPS.

c. Key Management

- Use centralized key management solutions like AWS Key Management Service (KMS), Azure Key Vault, or Google Cloud KMS.

- Rotate encryption keys regularly to minimize the impact of potential key exposure.

d. End-to-End Encryption (E2EE)

- Ensure data remains encrypted throughout its lifecycle, from the point of origin to the destination.

Best Practices:

- Encrypt sensitive fields in databases, such as personally identifiable information (PII).

- Implement disk-level encryption for storage devices.

- Use client-side encryption for additional protection.

---

2. Monitoring Tools

a. Importance of Monitoring

- Monitoring tools provide visibility into hybrid cloud environments, enabling organizations to detect and respond to threats in real-time.

b. Key Monitoring Metrics

- **Performance Metrics:** CPU usage, memory utilization, and network throughput.

- **Security Metrics:** Unauthorized access attempts, unusual traffic patterns, and failed login attempts.

- **Compliance Metrics:** Logs of data access and changes to configurations.

c. Common Monitoring Tools:

- **Cloud-Native Tools:**

  - AWS CloudWatch: Monitors AWS resources and applications.

  - Azure Monitor: Tracks Azure workloads and provides actionable insights.

  - Google Cloud Operations Suite: Offers logging, monitoring, and error reporting.

- **Third-Party Tools:**

  - Splunk: Provides real-time security analytics and log management.

  - Datadog: Monitors hybrid environments, integrating on-premises and cloud resources.

o Elastic Stack (ELK): Centralizes logs for analysis and visualization.

Best Practices:

- Implement real-time alerts for security incidents, such as unauthorized access or data exfiltration.

- Use machine learning to identify patterns indicative of advanced threats.

- Regularly audit logs to ensure they are comprehensive and actionable.

3. Intrusion Detection and Prevention Systems (IDS/IPS)

a. Role of IDS/IPS

- Intrusion Detection Systems (IDS) monitor networks for suspicious activity and generate alerts.

- Intrusion Prevention Systems (IPS) actively block malicious traffic based on predefined rules.

b. Examples of IDS/IPS Tools:

- Snort: Open-source network intrusion detection and prevention system.

- AWS Shield: Provides DDoS protection for AWS applications.

- Azure DDoS Protection: Mitigates DDoS attacks in Azure environments.

Case Study: Securing a Hybrid Cloud Deployment

Scenario:
A healthcare organization adopted a hybrid cloud to store patient records on-premises while using cloud platforms for analytics. The environment posed unique security challenges, including regulatory compliance with HIPAA and protecting sensitive data from cyberattacks.

Solution:

1. **Access Control:** Implemented Azure Active Directory with MFA and RBAC to secure user access.

2. **Encryption:** Deployed AWS KMS to encrypt data at rest and SSL/TLS for data in transit.

3. **Monitoring:** Used Datadog to monitor hybrid cloud performance and detect anomalies.

4. **Compliance:** Conducted regular audits using AWS CloudTrail to ensure compliance with HIPAA requirements.

Outcome:
The organization achieved a 40% reduction in security incidents, ensured HIPAA compliance, and improved visibility into its hybrid cloud operations.

Securing hybrid cloud environments requires a multi-faceted approach that includes identifying vulnerabilities, implementing robust access control and identity management, and leveraging encryption and monitoring tools. By adopting these strategies, organizations can protect their data, maintain compliance, and ensure the reliability of their hybrid cloud solutions.

In the next chapter, we will explore workload distribution and optimization strategies to maximize performance and cost-efficiency in hybrid cloud environments.

Chapter 10: Workload Distribution and Optimization

Hybrid cloud environments provide organizations with the flexibility to distribute workloads between on-premises infrastructure and cloud platforms, balancing performance, cost, scalability, and security. Efficient workload distribution is crucial for optimizing resource utilization and meeting business goals. This chapter explores how to decide which workloads to run on-premises versus in the cloud, the role of containerization and orchestration tools like Kubernetes, and strategies for performance optimization.

Deciding Which Workloads to Run On-Premises vs. in the Cloud

Determining the ideal placement of workloads in a hybrid cloud environment is a critical decision influenced by factors such as cost, latency, compliance, and application requirements.

1. Key Factors Influencing Workload Placement

a. Performance Requirements

- **Low Latency Needs:** Workloads requiring minimal latency, such as real-time analytics or IoT systems, are better suited for on-premises infrastructure.

- **Compute-Intensive Tasks:** High-performance computing (HPC) or AI workloads may benefit from cloud resources with specialized GPUs and scalability.

b. Data Sensitivity and Compliance

- Workloads handling sensitive data, such as personally identifiable information (PII) or health records, are often kept on-premises to ensure compliance with regulations like GDPR or HIPAA.

- Less sensitive workloads, like data processing or testing, can be offloaded to the cloud.

c. Scalability Requirements

- **Dynamic Workloads:** Applications with fluctuating demands, such as e-commerce websites, are ideal for cloud environments that offer elastic scalability.

- **Static Workloads:** Applications with consistent resource needs may remain on-premises for cost efficiency.

d. Cost Considerations

- Cloud resources operate on a pay-as-you-go model, making them cost-effective for temporary workloads but expensive for sustained, high-volume tasks.

- On-premises systems involve fixed costs, which can be advantageous for predictable workloads.

e. Dependency and Interoperability

- Applications with strong dependencies on legacy systems or specific hardware are typically run on-premises.

- Cloud-native workloads, designed with modern development frameworks, are more suitable for cloud deployment.

2. Workload Classification for Hybrid Cloud

a. On-Premises Workloads

- **Legacy Systems:** Applications that cannot be easily modernized or migrated.

- **Compliance-Critical Workloads:** Systems storing sensitive or regulated data.

- **Latency-Sensitive Applications:** Real-time operations like manufacturing systems.

b. Cloud Workloads

- **DevOps and Testing:** Development and testing environments that require scalability.

- **Big Data Analytics:** Data processing tasks requiring massive, temporary compute power.

- **Disaster Recovery:** Cloud-based backups for quick failover and recovery.

c. Hybrid Workloads

- Applications requiring both on-premises and cloud resources, such as multi-tier applications with a local database and cloud-based frontend.

3. Tools for Workload Assessment

- **AWS Migration Evaluator:** Provides insights into on-premises workloads to determine cost and performance benefits of moving to AWS.

- **Azure Migrate:** Assists with evaluating workloads for migration to Azure.

- **Google Cloud Migration Center:** Helps assess workloads for Google Cloud readiness.

Leveraging Containerization and Orchestration Tools like Kubernetes

Containerization and orchestration tools enable consistent, scalable, and portable workload management across hybrid cloud environments. These technologies simplify deployment and improve resource utilization.

1. Understanding Containerization

a. What Are Containers?
Containers package applications and their

dependencies into isolated environments, ensuring they run consistently across different systems.

b. Benefits of Containerization:

- **Portability:** Containers can run on any environment with a compatible container runtime, such as Docker.

- **Efficiency:** Containers share the host operating system, reducing resource overhead compared to virtual machines (VMs).

- **Scalability:** Containers can be easily replicated to handle increased demand.

c. Popular Containerization Tools:

- **Docker:** A leading platform for building, shipping, and running containers.

- **Podman:** An alternative container engine focused on security and compliance.

---

2. Orchestration with Kubernetes

a. What Is Kubernetes?

Kubernetes is an open-source container orchestration platform that automates the deployment, scaling, and management of containerized applications.

b. Key Features of Kubernetes:

- **Scaling:** Automatically adjusts the number of running containers based on workload demands.

- **Load Balancing:** Distributes traffic across containers to ensure availability and performance.

- **Self-Healing:** Detects and replaces failed containers automatically.

- **Resource Management:** Optimizes CPU and memory allocation for containers.

c. Kubernetes in Hybrid Cloud Environments:

- **Multi-Cluster Management:** Kubernetes enables organizations to manage clusters across on-premises and cloud environments.

- **Hybrid Deployments:** Applications can span multiple environments, leveraging the strengths of each.

d. Managed Kubernetes Services:

- **Amazon EKS (Elastic Kubernetes Service):** Kubernetes management on AWS.

- **Azure Kubernetes Service (AKS):** Kubernetes integration with Microsoft Azure.

- **Google Kubernetes Engine (GKE):** Fully managed Kubernetes on Google Cloud.

---

3. Best Practices for Using Kubernetes in Hybrid Clouds

- **Use Namespace Segmentation:** Organize workloads into namespaces for better management and security.

- **Enable Autoscaling:** Configure Kubernetes' horizontal pod autoscaler to match workload demands.

- **Integrate with CI/CD Pipelines:** Streamline deployment processes with tools like Jenkins or GitLab.

- **Monitor Kubernetes Clusters:** Use tools like Prometheus or Grafana for monitoring and visualization.

Strategies for Performance Optimization

Optimizing performance in a hybrid cloud environment ensures that workloads achieve their intended goals efficiently while minimizing costs.

1. Optimizing Workload Placement

a. Data Proximity:

- Place workloads close to the data they process to reduce latency and improve performance.

b. Resource Matching:

- Align workload requirements with the most suitable resources (e.g., CPU, memory, storage).

c. Real-Time Decision Making:

- Use dynamic workload placement tools that analyze performance metrics to move workloads between environments as needed.

2. Implementing Caching and Content Delivery

a. Caching:

- Cache frequently accessed data at the edge or in memory to improve response times.

b. Content Delivery Networks (CDNs):

- Use CDNs like Cloudflare or AWS CloudFront to deliver content from servers closer to end users.

---

3. Leveraging Edge Computing

Definition:
Edge computing processes data closer to its source, reducing latency and bandwidth usage.

Applications:

- IoT systems that require real-time data processing.

- AR/VR applications demanding low-latency interactions.

---

4. Monitoring and Performance Tuning

a. Monitoring Tools:

- **Cloud-Native:** AWS CloudWatch, Azure Monitor, Google Cloud Operations Suite.

- **Third-Party:** Datadog, New Relic, Splunk.

b. Key Metrics to Monitor:

- CPU and memory usage.

- Network latency and throughput.

- Storage I/O performance.

c. Performance Tuning:

- Optimize application code and database queries.

- Use load balancers to distribute traffic effectively.

- Configure auto-scaling to handle spikes in demand.

---

5. Cost Optimization Strategies

a. Right-Sizing:

- Allocate resources based on workload requirements to avoid overprovisioning.

b. Spot and Reserved Instances:

- Use spot instances for non-critical tasks and reserved instances for predictable workloads.

c. Multi-Cloud Strategies:

- Leverage cost advantages by running workloads on the most cost-effective platform.

Case Study: Optimizing Workload Distribution in a Hybrid Cloud

Scenario:
A global e-commerce company wanted to optimize its hybrid cloud setup to handle seasonal demand spikes while minimizing costs and maintaining performance.

Solution:

1. **Workload Placement:** Customer-facing applications were hosted in the cloud for scalability, while the inventory management system remained on-premises for low latency.

2. **Containerization:** Docker containers were used for microservices, improving portability and deployment speed.

3. **Orchestration:** Kubernetes was deployed to automate scaling and manage workloads across on-premises and cloud clusters.

4. **Performance Optimization:** CDNs cached static content, and load balancers distributed traffic across multiple regions.

5. **Monitoring:** Datadog was implemented to track performance and identify bottlenecks.

Outcome:
The company achieved a 30% reduction in costs, 40% improvement in application performance, and the ability to scale seamlessly during peak periods.

Efficient workload distribution and optimization are central to maximizing the value of hybrid cloud environments. By strategically placing workloads, leveraging containerization and orchestration tools like Kubernetes, and employing performance optimization strategies, organizations can achieve a balance of cost, performance, and scalability.

In the next chapter, we will explore automation in hybrid cloud environments, focusing on tools and practices for streamlining operations and reducing complexity.

Chapter 11: Automation in Hybrid Cloud Environments

Automation is the cornerstone of modern hybrid cloud management, streamlining processes, improving consistency, and reducing operational overhead. Hybrid cloud environments, with their complexity and dynamic nature, benefit greatly from automation tools and practices that ensure seamless deployment, configuration, and management. This chapter explores how to automate deployment using Infrastructure as Code (IaC), implement configuration management and CI/CD pipelines, and reduce operational overhead through strategic automation.

Automating Deployment with Infrastructure as Code (IaC)

Infrastructure as Code (IaC) revolutionizes the way IT infrastructure is provisioned and managed. By treating infrastructure configurations as code, organizations can automate the deployment of resources across hybrid cloud environments with precision and consistency.

---

1. What Is Infrastructure as Code (IaC)?

Definition:
IaC is the process of managing and provisioning infrastructure using machine-readable configuration files, rather than manual processes. These files describe the desired state of infrastructure, which automation tools then implement.

Benefits of IaC:

- **Consistency:** Eliminates human error by standardizing infrastructure configurations.

- **Speed:** Automates repetitive tasks, reducing time to deploy resources.

- **Version Control:** Treating configurations as code allows tracking changes, rollback to previous states, and collaborative editing.

- **Scalability:** IaC makes scaling resources up or down seamless and efficient.

---

2. Common IaC Tools for Hybrid Cloud Environments

a. Terraform

- **Overview:** An open-source tool by HashiCorp, Terraform supports multiple cloud providers and on-premises systems.

- **Use Cases:** Provisioning virtual machines, storage, and networking across AWS, Azure, Google Cloud, and more.

- **Key Features:** Declarative syntax, resource state management, and multi-cloud compatibility.

b. AWS CloudFormation

- **Overview:** A native AWS IaC tool that automates the provisioning of AWS resources.

- **Use Cases:** Managing complex AWS environments with integrated service support.

- **Key Features:** YAML/JSON templates and seamless integration with AWS services.

c. Azure Resource Manager (ARM) Templates

- **Overview:** A Microsoft Azure-specific IaC tool for managing Azure resources.

- **Use Cases:** Deploying and managing infrastructure in Azure environments.

- **Key Features:** Declarative templates and integration with Azure DevOps.

d. Google Cloud Deployment Manager

- **Overview:** Google Cloud's native IaC tool for resource deployment.

- **Use Cases:** Automating resource provisioning within Google Cloud environments.

- **Key Features:** YAML configuration and support for multi-region deployments.

---

3. IaC Best Practices

a. Modular Configuration Files:

- Break configurations into smaller, reusable modules to simplify management.

- Example: Separate files for networking, compute, and storage resources.

b. Version Control Integration:

- Use Git or other version control systems to manage IaC files.

- Benefits: Collaboration, change tracking, and rollback capabilities.

c. Testing Infrastructure:

- Test configurations in staging environments before deploying to production.

- Use tools like Terratest for automated IaC testing.

d. Idempotency:

- Ensure that running IaC scripts multiple times does not lead to unintended changes.

Tools for Configuration Management and CI/CD Pipelines

Configuration management and Continuous Integration/Continuous Deployment (CI/CD) pipelines are critical for managing hybrid cloud environments effectively. These tools automate application delivery and ensure that infrastructure and applications remain consistent.

1. Configuration Management Tools

a. What Is Configuration Management?

Configuration management involves maintaining the desired state of IT infrastructure, ensuring that resources are configured consistently across environments.

b. Popular Tools:

i. Ansible

- **Overview:** A powerful, agentless configuration management tool that uses YAML playbooks.

- **Key Features:** Simplified syntax, broad compatibility, and seamless hybrid cloud integration.

- **Use Cases:** Installing software, configuring network devices, and automating routine tasks.

ii. Chef

- **Overview:** A configuration management tool that uses code (recipes) to define system states.

- **Key Features:** Scalability, support for hybrid environments, and integration with CI/CD pipelines.

- **Use Cases:** Managing server configurations and ensuring consistent environments.

iii. Puppet

- **Overview:** A declarative configuration management tool that automates infrastructure provisioning.

- **Key Features:** Centralized management, reporting capabilities, and multi-environment support.

- **Use Cases:** Managing complex, large-scale hybrid cloud environments.

---

2. Continuous Integration/Continuous Deployment (CI/CD) Pipelines

a. What Are CI/CD Pipelines?

CI/CD pipelines automate the process of building, testing, and deploying applications. They ensure rapid delivery while maintaining code quality and minimizing errors.

b. Benefits of CI/CD in Hybrid Clouds:

- Faster application delivery.

- Reduced deployment errors.

- Seamless updates across on-premises and cloud environments.

c. Popular CI/CD Tools:

i. Jenkins

- **Overview:** An open-source automation server for building, testing, and deploying applications.

- **Key Features:** Plugin ecosystem, pipeline-as-code, and hybrid cloud integration.

- **Use Cases:** Automating build and deployment processes across environments.

ii. GitLab CI/CD

- **Overview:** A CI/CD platform integrated with GitLab for version control and collaboration.

- **Key Features:** Built-in pipelines, Kubernetes integration, and monitoring tools.

- **Use Cases:** Deploying microservices in hybrid environments.

iii. AWS CodePipeline

- **Overview:** AWS's CI/CD service for automating application deployment.

- **Key Features:** Integration with AWS services and third-party tools.

- **Use Cases:** Streamlining deployments in AWS-based hybrid setups.

iv. Azure DevOps

- **Overview:** A suite of development tools for CI/CD pipelines in Microsoft Azure.

- **Key Features:** Multi-cloud compatibility, extensive templates, and monitoring capabilities.

- **Use Cases:** Managing complex CI/CD pipelines across hybrid environments.

---

3. Integrating Configuration Management and CI/CD

a. Combining Tools:

- Use configuration management tools like Ansible to set up infrastructure and CI/CD tools like Jenkins to deploy applications.

b. Automation Workflows:

- Automate provisioning, configuration, testing, and deployment as part of a unified workflow.

c. Monitoring Pipelines:

- Monitor CI/CD pipelines to identify bottlenecks and improve efficiency using tools like Datadog or Prometheus.

Reducing Operational Overhead Through Automation

Automation not only simplifies processes but also reduces the time and resources required for managing hybrid cloud environments.

1. Automating Routine Tasks

a. Patch Management:

- Use tools like WSUS (Windows Server Update Services) or Ansible to automate software updates and patches.

b. Scaling Resources:

- Leverage auto-scaling features in cloud platforms to adjust resource allocation based on demand.

c. Backup and Disaster Recovery:

- Automate backup processes and disaster recovery drills using tools like AWS Backup or Azure Site Recovery.

2. Monitoring and Self-Healing Systems

a. Automated Monitoring:

- Deploy monitoring tools like AWS CloudWatch or Splunk to track performance and detect anomalies.

b. Self-Healing Mechanisms:

- Configure orchestration tools like Kubernetes to replace failed containers automatically.

- Implement scripts to restart services or redeploy resources in case of failures.

---

3. Cost Optimization Through Automation

a. Resource Scheduling:

- Automate the shutdown of unused resources during off-peak hours to reduce costs.

b. Right-Sizing Resources:

- Use tools like AWS Cost Explorer or Azure Cost Management to analyze resource usage and optimize allocations.

c. Spot Instances:

- Automate the use of spot instances for non-critical tasks to take advantage of cost savings.

---

4. Security Automation

a. Automated Threat Detection:

- Use tools like AWS GuardDuty or Azure Security Center to identify and respond to threats in real-time.

b. Policy Enforcement:

- Automate security policy enforcement using tools like HashiCorp Sentinel or Open Policy Agent (OPA).

Case Study: Automating a Hybrid Cloud Environment

Scenario:
A global media company faced challenges managing its hybrid cloud environment, including inconsistent deployments, high operational costs, and slow application delivery.

Solution:

1. **IaC Deployment:** The company implemented Terraform to automate infrastructure provisioning across AWS and on-premises systems.

2. **Configuration Management:** Ansible was used to standardize server configurations and manage updates.

3. **CI/CD Pipelines:** Jenkins pipelines were deployed to automate application builds, tests, and deployments.

4. **Monitoring and Self-Healing:** Kubernetes monitored container health and replaced failed pods automatically.

5. **Cost Optimization:** Auto-scaling policies and spot instances reduced costs by 25%.

Outcome:
The company achieved faster deployments, improved resource utilization, and reduced operational overhead, enabling teams to focus on innovation rather than maintenance.

Automation is a game-changer for hybrid cloud environments, enabling organizations to deploy resources efficiently, maintain consistency, and reduce operational complexity. By leveraging Infrastructure as Code, configuration management tools, and CI/CD pipelines, businesses can achieve scalable, secure, and cost-effective operations.

In the next chapter, we will explore hybrid cloud monitoring and analytics, focusing on tools and techniques for gaining real-time insights and optimizing performance.

Chapter 12: Hybrid Cloud Monitoring and Analytics

Monitoring and analytics are essential to maintaining the performance, security, and efficiency of hybrid cloud environments. As hybrid cloud infrastructures grow in complexity, businesses must adopt advanced tools and strategies to track infrastructure health, gain predictive insights, and make data-driven decisions. This chapter explores the tools available for monitoring hybrid cloud environments, the role of Artificial Intelligence for IT Operations (AIOps) in predictive analytics, and techniques for visualizing metrics to support informed decision-making.

Tools for Monitoring Infrastructure Health and Performance

Effective hybrid cloud monitoring requires tools that provide real-time insights into the health, performance, and security of both on-premises and cloud environments. These tools enable proactive issue resolution, resource optimization, and compliance management.

---

1. Categories of Monitoring Tools

a. Infrastructure Monitoring Tools

- Monitor the performance and availability of compute, storage, and network resources.

- Key Metrics: CPU utilization, disk I/O, network latency, and memory usage.

b. Application Performance Monitoring (APM) Tools

- Track application behavior, response times, and user experience.

- Key Metrics: Application latency, error rates, and transaction throughput.

c. Security Monitoring Tools

- Detect and prevent unauthorized access, data breaches, and other threats.

- Key Metrics: Intrusion attempts, firewall logs, and data access patterns.

d. End-to-End Monitoring Tools

- Provide a unified view of hybrid cloud environments, integrating infrastructure, applications, and security data.

---

2. Popular Monitoring Tools for Hybrid Cloud

a. Cloud-Native Monitoring Tools

- **AWS CloudWatch:** Monitors AWS resources and applications, offering alarms and dashboards for tracking key metrics.

- **Azure Monitor:** Provides comprehensive monitoring for Azure environments, with features like log analytics and application insights.

- **Google Cloud Operations Suite:** Tracks Google Cloud resources and applications, supporting logs, traces, and error reporting.

b. Third-Party Monitoring Tools

- **Datadog:** A cloud-based platform offering infrastructure monitoring, APM, and log management for hybrid and multi-cloud environments.

- **New Relic:** Provides APM and infrastructure monitoring with AI-driven insights and customizable dashboards.

- **Splunk:** An analytics platform that centralizes log data from on-premises and cloud systems for monitoring and troubleshooting.

c. Open-Source Monitoring Tools

- **Prometheus:** A powerful tool for monitoring and alerting, particularly well-suited for containerized environments.

- **ELK Stack (Elasticsearch, Logstash, Kibana):** Combines log collection, indexing, and visualization for a unified monitoring experience.

- **Zabbix:** A versatile open-source tool that monitors infrastructure and applications.

3. Best Practices for Hybrid Cloud Monitoring

a. Centralized Monitoring:

- Use a unified platform to monitor on-premises and cloud resources, reducing complexity and enabling a holistic view.

b. Proactive Alerting:

- Set up real-time alerts for critical metrics, such as high CPU usage or network downtime, to address issues before they impact operations.

c. Regular Performance Audits:

- Periodically review performance data to identify trends and optimize resource allocation.

d. Integration with ITSM Tools:

- Connect monitoring tools with IT Service Management (ITSM) systems like ServiceNow to streamline incident response workflows.

Using AIOps for Predictive Insights

Artificial Intelligence for IT Operations (AIOps) combines machine learning, big data, and analytics to enhance IT operations. In hybrid cloud environments, AIOps can predict potential issues, automate resolutions, and optimize performance.

1. What Is AIOps?

Definition:
AIOps refers to the use of AI and machine learning to analyze IT data, identify patterns, and provide actionable insights for managing infrastructure and applications.

Key Capabilities of AIOps:

- **Anomaly Detection:** Identifies unusual patterns or behaviors in metrics, such as sudden spikes in latency.

- **Predictive Analytics:** Forecasts future resource usage and potential failures based on historical data.

- **Automated Incident Response:** Suggests or executes solutions to common issues without manual intervention.

- **Noise Reduction:** Filters irrelevant alerts, focusing on meaningful incidents to reduce alert fatigue.

2. AIOps in Hybrid Cloud Environments

a. Predicting Resource Demands:

- AIOps tools analyze historical workload data to predict future demands, enabling proactive scaling and cost optimization.

b. Identifying Root Causes:

- By correlating logs, metrics, and events, AIOps helps pinpoint the root cause of performance issues, speeding up resolution.

c. Enhancing Security:

- Detects and responds to potential security threats, such as unusual login attempts or unauthorized data access.

d. Supporting Multi-Cloud Management:

- AIOps tools simplify the management of multi-cloud and hybrid environments by providing a unified view and actionable insights across platforms.

3. Popular AIOps Tools

a. Splunk IT Service Intelligence (ITSI):

- Features AI-driven insights, predictive analytics, and root cause analysis for hybrid cloud environments.

b. Dynatrace:

- Offers AI-powered application and infrastructure monitoring with automated root cause analysis.

c. IBM Watson AIOps:

- Uses natural language processing (NLP) and machine learning to detect anomalies and automate incident management.

d. Moogsoft:

- Focuses on reducing alert noise and accelerating incident resolution using AI and machine learning.

---

4. Benefits of AIOps in Hybrid Cloud

- **Proactive Maintenance:** Identifies and addresses potential issues before they impact users.

- **Increased Efficiency:** Automates repetitive tasks, freeing IT teams for strategic initiatives.

- **Improved Performance:** Optimizes resource allocation and application performance based on predictive insights.

- **Enhanced Security:** Detects threats in real-time, reducing the risk of breaches.

Visualizing Hybrid Cloud Metrics for Informed Decision-Making

Visualization is a critical aspect of hybrid cloud monitoring and analytics. Clear and intuitive dashboards help IT teams understand complex data, identify trends, and make informed decisions.

1. Importance of Visualization

a. Simplifies Complex Data:

- Converts raw metrics into actionable insights through charts, graphs, and heatmaps.

b. Enhances Collaboration:

- Provides a shared view for IT teams and stakeholders, improving communication and decision-making.

c. Speeds Up Issue Resolution:

- Highlights anomalies and bottlenecks, enabling quick responses.

2. Key Metrics to Visualize

a. Infrastructure Metrics:

- CPU utilization, memory usage, disk I/O, and network performance.

b. Application Metrics:

- Response times, error rates, and user activity.

c. Security Metrics:

- Failed login attempts, firewall activity, and data access logs.

d. Financial Metrics:

- Cloud resource costs, unused resources, and cost optimization opportunities.

3. Tools for Visualizing Hybrid Cloud Metrics

a. Kibana (ELK Stack):

- Offers customizable dashboards for visualizing data collected by Elasticsearch.

b. Grafana:

- Integrates with multiple data sources (Prometheus, InfluxDB, AWS CloudWatch) to create detailed visualizations.

c. Microsoft Power BI:

- Transforms hybrid cloud data into interactive reports and dashboards.

d. Tableau:

- Provides advanced data visualization tools for analyzing hybrid cloud performance and cost metrics.

---

4. Best Practices for Visualization

a. Customize Dashboards:

- Tailor dashboards to focus on metrics relevant to specific teams or roles.

- Example: An application team may prioritize response times, while a security team focuses on access logs.

b. Use Threshold Alerts:

- Configure visual indicators (e.g., red/yellow/green) to highlight critical metrics and thresholds.

c. Correlate Metrics Across Layers:

- Display metrics from infrastructure, applications, and security on a single dashboard to identify interdependencies.

d. Regularly Update Dashboards:

- Ensure visualizations reflect the current hybrid cloud architecture and priorities.

Case Study: Monitoring and Analytics in a Hybrid Cloud

Scenario:
A global financial services company struggled to monitor its hybrid cloud environment, resulting in frequent performance bottlenecks and compliance issues.

Solution:

1. **Centralized Monitoring:** Implemented Datadog for unified monitoring of on-premises and cloud resources.

2. **AIOps Deployment:** Used IBM Watson AIOps to predict resource demands and automate incident resolution.

3. **Custom Dashboards:** Created Grafana dashboards to visualize metrics like application latency, CPU utilization, and security events.

4. **Proactive Alerts:** Configured alerts for critical thresholds, such as disk space nearing capacity.

Outcome:
The company reduced downtime by 40%, improved application performance, and achieved real-time compliance monitoring, ensuring adherence to regulations like GDPR.

Hybrid cloud monitoring and analytics are vital for maintaining a resilient, efficient, and secure IT environment. By using robust tools, leveraging AIOps for predictive insights, and visualizing metrics effectively, organizations can gain real-time visibility, optimize performance, and make data-driven decisions.

In the next chapter, we will explore real-world applications of hybrid cloud technology, showcasing case studies from various industries and the lessons learned from their implementations.

Chapter 13: Real-World Applications of Hybrid Cloud

Hybrid cloud solutions are reshaping industries by providing flexible, scalable, and secure IT infrastructure tailored to diverse needs. From improving healthcare outcomes to streamlining manufacturing processes, hybrid cloud empowers organizations to innovate, optimize, and grow. This chapter explores real-world applications of hybrid cloud across various industries, examines case studies of successful implementations, and distills lessons learned from practical experiences.

Examples from Industries

Hybrid cloud's adaptability makes it invaluable across sectors. Here's how various industries leverage its capabilities:

1. Healthcare

The healthcare sector requires secure, compliant, and efficient systems to manage sensitive patient data and enable advanced medical research. Hybrid cloud solutions address these needs by balancing on-premises control with cloud scalability.

Applications:

- **Electronic Health Records (EHR):** Store sensitive patient data on-premises for compliance while leveraging the cloud for analytics and insights.

- **Telemedicine:** Use cloud-based platforms to provide remote consultations and manage patient interactions.

- **Medical Research:** Employ cloud computing for genome sequencing and drug discovery, requiring high-performance resources.

Example:
A hospital group uses a hybrid cloud to process MRI data on-premises and share anonymized data with researchers in the cloud for AI-driven analysis.

2. Finance

Financial institutions need robust systems to manage transactions, comply with regulations, and combat cyber threats. Hybrid cloud solutions offer secure and scalable platforms to meet these demands.

Applications:

- **Fraud Detection:** Use AI-powered tools in the cloud to analyze transaction patterns while keeping sensitive customer data on-premises.

- **Trading Platforms:** Host trading algorithms in the cloud for low-latency execution, with on-premises backup systems for resilience.

- **Regulatory Compliance:** Maintain data sovereignty by storing regulated data locally while processing it in compliant cloud environments.

Example:
A global bank employs a hybrid cloud to run real-time fraud detection algorithms in the cloud while storing transaction logs on-premises to meet compliance requirements.

3. Manufacturing

Manufacturers adopt hybrid cloud to optimize operations, improve product quality, and enhance supply chain visibility.

Applications:

- **IoT Integration:** Connect factory-floor sensors to on-premises systems for real-time monitoring while analyzing trends in the cloud.

- **Supply Chain Management:** Use cloud platforms to predict demand, optimize inventory, and reduce costs.

- **Quality Assurance:** Apply AI models in the cloud to detect defects using images captured by on-premises cameras.

Example:
A car manufacturer integrates IoT devices across factories with cloud-based analytics to predict machine failures and reduce downtime.

---

4. Retail and E-Commerce

Retailers leverage hybrid cloud to deliver seamless customer experiences, scale during peak demand, and gain insights into consumer behavior.

Applications:

- **Personalized Shopping:** Use cloud-based AI to analyze customer preferences and suggest personalized product recommendations.

- **Dynamic Scalability:** Handle high traffic during sales events by scaling e-commerce platforms into the cloud.

- **Inventory Management:** Combine on-premises systems for local stock tracking with cloud analytics for demand forecasting.

Example:
An online retailer uses a hybrid cloud to scale its website during Black Friday sales while keeping payment processing systems on-premises for enhanced security.

---

5. Education

Educational institutions adopt hybrid cloud to support online learning, enhance administrative efficiency, and facilitate research.

Applications:

- **E-Learning Platforms:** Host video lectures and course materials in the cloud while managing student data on-premises.

- **Administrative Systems:** Use hybrid solutions to streamline admissions, payroll, and scheduling.

- **Research Collaboration:** Enable researchers to share and analyze data globally through secure cloud platforms.

Example:
A university integrates on-premises databases with cloud-based e-learning tools to support remote education during a pandemic.

Case Studies of Successful Hybrid Cloud Implementations

Let's explore detailed examples of organizations that have implemented hybrid cloud strategies effectively.

Case Study 1: Healthcare Organization Optimizing Patient Care

Organization: A regional healthcare provider with multiple hospitals and clinics.

Challenge:

- Manage growing volumes of sensitive patient data.

- Comply with HIPAA regulations.

- Enable remote patient monitoring and telemedicine services.

Solution:

- Stored EHRs on-premises to maintain compliance.

- Deployed a cloud-based telemedicine platform for remote consultations.

- Used a hybrid cloud to analyze aggregated patient data, enabling predictive healthcare analytics.

Outcome:

- Reduced patient wait times by 30%.

- Improved diagnostic accuracy through AI-driven analytics.

- Ensured compliance with HIPAA while enabling innovation.

Lesson Learned:
Hybrid cloud can balance stringent regulatory

requirements with the need for scalable, innovative services in healthcare.

Case Study 2: Financial Institution Enhancing Fraud Prevention

Organization: A global bank operating in multiple countries.

Challenge:

- Detect fraudulent activities in real-time.

- Store sensitive financial data securely to comply with regulations.

- Ensure seamless operations across global branches.

Solution:

- Hosted fraud detection algorithms on a cloud platform for rapid analysis.

- Retained customer transaction data on-premises to comply with data sovereignty laws.

- Established direct connections between on-premises data centers and the cloud to reduce latency.

Outcome:

- Detected and prevented fraud in milliseconds, reducing losses by 40%.

- Improved customer trust with enhanced data security.

- Achieved compliance with local and international regulations.

Lesson Learned:
Hybrid cloud facilitates secure, real-time analytics essential for combating financial fraud while ensuring compliance.

Case Study 3: Manufacturer Boosting Operational Efficiency

Organization: A multinational manufacturing company.

Challenge:

- Minimize production downtime caused by equipment failures.

- Manage data generated by thousands of IoT sensors.

- Integrate global operations into a centralized system.

Solution:

- Deployed on-premises systems for real-time monitoring of factory-floor sensors.

- Sent aggregated data to the cloud for predictive maintenance analytics.

- Integrated ERP systems across locations into a hybrid cloud.

Outcome:

- Reduced machine downtime by 50% through predictive maintenance.

- Optimized inventory management, lowering costs by 20%.

- Improved operational visibility across global facilities.

Lesson Learned:
Hybrid cloud enables manufacturers to harness IoT data for predictive insights while maintaining robust on-premises control.

Case Study 4: Retailer Scaling for Seasonal Demand

Organization: A leading e-commerce company.

Challenge:

- Handle traffic surges during major sales events.
- Deliver personalized shopping experiences.
- Secure payment transactions against cyber threats.

Solution:

- Used cloud platforms to scale front-end applications dynamically during sales.
- Implemented AI-driven recommendation engines in the cloud.
- Maintained on-premises payment processing systems for enhanced security.

Outcome:

- Achieved 99.99% uptime during peak sales periods.
- Boosted sales by 25% through personalized shopping experiences.
- Enhanced customer trust with secure payment processing.

Lesson Learned:
Hybrid cloud provides the scalability needed to handle e-commerce surges while ensuring transaction security.

Lessons Learned from Real-World Scenarios

Organizations that have implemented hybrid cloud strategies share valuable insights that can guide others in their cloud journey:

1. Assess Workload Placement Carefully

- Analyze the specific needs of workloads, such as latency, compliance, and scalability, before deciding where to run them.

- Example: A financial firm kept sensitive data on-premises while offloading computationally intensive tasks to the cloud.

2. Prioritize Security and Compliance

- Adopt robust encryption, access controls, and monitoring to protect data across environments.

- Example: A healthcare provider ensured HIPAA compliance by keeping patient data on-premises while processing analytics in the cloud.

3. Optimize Costs with Hybrid Solutions

- Use on-premises systems for predictable workloads and cloud platforms for variable demands.

- Example: An e-commerce retailer reduced costs by scaling cloud resources during seasonal peaks.

4. Leverage Cloud-Native Tools

- Use cloud-native services, such as AI and big data platforms, to enhance innovation and efficiency.

- Example: A manufacturing company used cloud-based AI to predict equipment failures, saving millions in downtime costs.

5. Monitor and Adjust Continuously

- Implement real-time monitoring tools to track performance, detect anomalies, and optimize resource usage.

- Example: A global logistics firm used hybrid cloud monitoring to improve delivery times by 20%.

Hybrid cloud solutions empower organizations across industries to innovate, optimize operations, and meet unique challenges. By learning from real-world applications and case studies, businesses can develop strategies that harness the full potential of hybrid cloud technology while avoiding common pitfalls.

In the next chapter, we will explore managing hybrid cloud costs, offering strategies and tools to optimize spending and maximize ROI.

Chapter 14: Managing Hybrid Cloud Costs

Hybrid cloud environments offer the flexibility to leverage both on-premises and cloud resources, but they can also lead to unexpected and escalating costs if not managed effectively. Understanding cost drivers, implementing optimization strategies, and using the right tools for tracking and management are essential for achieving cost efficiency in hybrid cloud operations. This chapter explores cloud cost optimization strategies, tools for cost tracking, and best practices for balancing on-premises and cloud resource usage.

Cloud Cost Optimization Strategies

Cost optimization in a hybrid cloud environment involves analyzing resource usage, eliminating waste, and aligning expenditures with business objectives. Effective strategies can significantly reduce unnecessary costs while maximizing the value of hybrid cloud investments.

1. Rightsizing Resources

Definition:
Rightsizing involves aligning the size and type of resources with the actual workload requirements to avoid overprovisioning.

Key Steps for Rightsizing:

- Monitor resource usage over time to identify underutilized or oversized instances.

- Use cloud-native tools like AWS Compute Optimizer, Azure Advisor, or Google Cloud Recommender to receive recommendations for optimal resource configurations.

- Regularly review and adjust resource allocations based on workload changes.

Example:
A company running a web application identifies that its cloud servers are consistently operating at only 30% CPU utilization. By downgrading to smaller instances, they save 25% on monthly costs.

2. Implementing Auto-Scaling

Definition:
Auto-scaling dynamically adjusts cloud resources based on demand, ensuring optimal performance without overprovisioning.

Key Considerations for Auto-Scaling:

- Set thresholds for scaling up and down based on metrics like CPU usage, memory utilization, or request rates.

- Use predictive scaling to anticipate traffic spikes during peak periods.

- Combine auto-scaling with load balancing for seamless traffic distribution.

Example:
An e-commerce site uses auto-scaling to handle surges in traffic during holiday sales, avoiding both downtime and unnecessary costs during off-peak hours.

---

3. Optimizing Storage Costs

Storage optimization is a critical component of cost management:

- **Data Tiering:** Store frequently accessed data (hot data) in high-performance storage while archiving infrequently accessed data (cold data) in cheaper tiers.

- **Compression and Deduplication:** Reduce storage costs by minimizing data size.

- **Lifecycle Policies:** Automate data movement between storage tiers based on access patterns.

Example:
A healthcare organization saves 30% on storage costs by archiving older patient records to Amazon S3 Glacier while keeping recent records in high-speed storage.

4. Leveraging Reserved and Spot Instances

a. Reserved Instances (RIs):

- Commit to using specific cloud resources for a one- or three-year term in exchange for significant discounts.

- Ideal for predictable workloads like databases or core applications.

b. Spot Instances:

- Use spare cloud capacity offered at a discount, suitable for fault-tolerant or non-critical workloads.

- Example: Batch processing, big data analytics, or development and testing environments.

Example:
A media company saves 40% on rendering costs by using spot instances for non-time-sensitive video processing tasks.

---

5. Adopting Multi-Cloud Strategies

Definition:
Multi-cloud strategies involve leveraging multiple cloud providers to take advantage of competitive pricing and avoid vendor lock-in.

Key Considerations:

- Use tools like HashiCorp Terraform to manage resources across providers.

- Regularly compare pricing models and switch workloads to the most cost-effective platform.

Example:
A company splits workloads between AWS for compute-intensive tasks and Google Cloud for machine learning to optimize costs.

---

6. Managing Data Transfer Costs

Challenges:
Data transfer between on-premises systems and cloud platforms, or between clouds, can incur significant costs.

Solutions:

- Minimize data movement by processing data closer to its source.

- Use dedicated connections like AWS Direct Connect or Azure ExpressRoute for cost-effective transfers.

- Compress and batch data transfers to reduce bandwidth usage.

Example:
A logistics firm saves 20% on data transfer costs by processing IoT sensor data locally before sending summarized results to the cloud.

---

7. Implementing Governance Policies

Cost Governance Best Practices:

- Set budgets and enforce spending limits using tools like AWS Budgets or Azure Cost Management.

- Tag resources to track and allocate costs to specific teams or projects.

- Automate the decommissioning of unused resources to prevent unnecessary expenses.

Example:
A software company tags resources by project and automatically shuts down idle development environments overnight, saving 15% on monthly cloud bills.

Tools for Cost Tracking and Management

Effectively managing hybrid cloud costs requires visibility into resource usage and spending across on-premises and cloud environments. Numerous tools are available to help organizations monitor and optimize their expenditures.

---

1. Cloud-Native Cost Management Tools

a. AWS Cost Management Suite

- **Key Features:**
    - AWS Cost Explorer for analyzing spending trends.

- AWS Budgets for setting cost thresholds and receiving alerts.

- AWS Trusted Advisor for identifying cost-saving opportunities.

- **Use Case:** Track and optimize AWS resource usage with detailed insights and recommendations.

b. Azure Cost Management + Billing

- **Key Features:**

  - Unified view of Azure and on-premises spending.

  - Budget creation and anomaly detection.

  - Cost-saving recommendations via Azure Advisor.

- **Use Case:** Optimize Azure workloads with cost analysis and alerts.

c. Google Cloud Billing

- **Key Features:**

  - Detailed cost reports and dashboards.

  - Integration with BigQuery for advanced cost analysis.

  - Alerts for budget thresholds.

- **Use Case:** Monitor and forecast Google Cloud expenditures with precision.

---

2. Third-Party Cost Management Tools

a. CloudHealth by VMware

- Provides cost management, governance, and optimization insights across multi-cloud environments.

- Features detailed reporting, policy automation, and budget tracking.

b. Spot.io

- Specializes in optimizing cloud infrastructure costs by automating the use of spot instances and reserved capacity.

c. Apptio Cloudability

- Offers visibility into multi-cloud spending and provides recommendations for cost optimization.

---

3. Open-Source Tools

a. Kubecost

- Monitors and optimizes Kubernetes resource usage, providing cost insights for containerized workloads.

b. Prometheus + Grafana

- Tracks resource utilization and cost metrics, allowing customized dashboards for hybrid cloud environments.

---

4. Cost Reporting and Forecasting

a. Custom Dashboards:

- Use tools like Power BI or Tableau to create dashboards integrating on-premises and cloud cost data for holistic analysis.

b. Forecasting:

- Predict future spending using historical trends and workload patterns.

Balancing On-Premises vs. Cloud Resource Usage

Hybrid cloud environments thrive on the strategic balance between on-premises and cloud resources. Striking this balance ensures cost efficiency while meeting performance and compliance requirements.

---

1. When to Use On-Premises Resources

Ideal Scenarios:

- **Predictable Workloads:** Stable, long-term workloads that require consistent resource allocation.

- **Compliance Requirements:** Data that must remain on-premises for regulatory reasons.

- **Latency-Sensitive Applications:** Applications that require real-time processing with minimal delays.

Advantages:

- Lower costs for consistent workloads.

- Greater control over infrastructure.

- Reduced latency for local applications.

---

2. When to Use Cloud Resources

Ideal Scenarios:

- **Dynamic Workloads:** Applications with fluctuating demands, such as seasonal traffic spikes.

- **Development and Testing:** Temporary environments that can be easily provisioned and decommissioned.

- **Global Reach:** Applications requiring scalability across multiple regions.

Advantages:

- Elastic scalability.

- Access to advanced cloud-native tools (e.g., AI, big data).

- Reduced capital expenditures.

---

3. Hybrid Workloads

Examples of Hybrid Workloads:

- **Multi-Tier Applications:** Backend databases remain on-premises while front-end applications are hosted in the cloud.

- **Disaster Recovery:** On-premises systems act as the primary environment, with the cloud serving as a backup or failover location.

4. Optimizing Resource Allocation

Best Practices:

- Use workload assessment tools like Azure Migrate or AWS Migration Evaluator to determine the optimal placement of resources.

- Periodically reevaluate resource allocation based on performance and cost data.

- Establish clear policies for workload placement to avoid inefficiencies.

Case Study: Hybrid Cloud Cost Management Success

Scenario:
A global retail chain operates a hybrid cloud to support e-commerce, inventory management, and data analytics.

Challenge:
Escalating cloud costs due to underutilized resources and inefficient workload distribution.

Solution:

1. **Rightsizing:** Adjusted cloud instances based on actual usage, saving $500,000 annually.

2. **Auto-Scaling:** Implemented auto-scaling for e-commerce applications, reducing overprovisioning during off-peak hours.

3. **Data Tiering:** Moved archived inventory data to low-cost storage tiers, cutting storage costs by 40%.

4. **Monitoring:** Used CloudHealth to track spending trends and identify cost-saving opportunities.

5. **On-Premises Optimization:** Shifted predictable workloads to on-premises servers, reducing cloud reliance.

Outcome:
The company achieved a 25% reduction in overall IT costs while maintaining performance and scalability.

Managing hybrid cloud costs requires a proactive approach that combines rightsizing, automation, governance, and the use of advanced cost management tools. By balancing on-premises and cloud resource usage effectively, organizations can optimize their hybrid cloud environments for both performance and cost-efficiency.

In the next chapter, we will address the challenges of hybrid cloud adoption and provide strategies to overcome them.

Chapter 15: Addressing Challenges in Hybrid Cloud Adoption

Adopting a hybrid cloud strategy offers numerous benefits, such as flexibility, scalability, and cost efficiency. However, the journey to a successful hybrid cloud deployment is not without challenges. Organizations face technical, operational, and cultural hurdles that can slow down adoption or lead to suboptimal outcomes if not addressed proactively. This chapter explores common integration pitfalls, strategies to overcome organizational resistance and skill gaps, and techniques for fostering seamless collaboration between teams in a hybrid cloud environment.

Common Integration Pitfalls and How to Avoid Them

Hybrid cloud environments require seamless integration of on-premises systems with one or more cloud platforms. Missteps during integration can lead to inefficiencies, security risks, and performance issues.

---

1. Incompatible Systems and Architectures

Challenge:
Legacy on-premises systems often lack compatibility with modern cloud architectures, leading to integration challenges.

Examples:

- Applications reliant on outdated operating systems.

- Proprietary hardware that cannot connect to cloud APIs.

Solution:

- **Modernization:** Upgrade legacy systems to ensure compatibility with cloud platforms.

- **Middleware:** Use middleware solutions or APIs to bridge compatibility gaps. Tools like MuleSoft or Apache Camel can simplify integration.

- **Hybrid Cloud-Ready Vendors:** Choose cloud vendors that offer hybrid-friendly services, such as AWS Outposts or Azure Stack.

2. Data Transfer and Synchronization Issues

Challenge:
Hybrid cloud environments often require data to be transferred between on-premises systems and the cloud. Mismanaged transfers can lead to data inconsistencies, latency, or loss.

Examples:

- Data corruption during synchronization.

- Excessive latency impacting application performance.

Solution:

- **Data Integration Tools:** Leverage tools like Azure Data Factory, AWS DataSync, or Google Cloud Transfer Service for secure and efficient data transfers.

- **Real-Time Synchronization:** Use streaming platforms like Apache Kafka for near-real-time synchronization.

- **Testing and Validation:** Perform thorough testing to ensure data integrity during transfers.

3. Security and Compliance Challenges

Challenge:
The distributed nature of hybrid cloud environments introduces additional attack surfaces and compliance risks.

Examples:

- Misconfigured cloud resources exposing sensitive data.

- Non-compliance with data sovereignty laws.

Solution:

- **Unified Security Policies:** Implement consistent security protocols across on-premises and cloud environments.

- **Compliance Tools:** Use tools like AWS Artifact or Azure Compliance Manager to ensure adherence to regulations.

- **Encryption:** Encrypt data in transit and at rest using industry standards such as AES-256.

---

4. Lack of Visibility Across Environments

Challenge:
Operating in a hybrid cloud can make it difficult to

maintain visibility into the performance and security of resources.

Examples:

- Delayed issue resolution due to fragmented monitoring.

- Inconsistent logging practices between environments.

Solution:

- **Centralized Monitoring:** Use tools like Datadog, Splunk, or Microsoft Sentinel to monitor and analyze metrics across all environments.

- **Unified Dashboards:** Create dashboards that display performance, security, and cost data in one place.

---

5. Overestimated Cost Savings

Challenge:
Organizations often underestimate the operational complexities of hybrid cloud and overestimate cost savings, leading to budget overruns.

Examples:

- Higher-than-expected data transfer costs.

- Inefficient workload distribution causing cloud resource overuse.

Solution:

- **Comprehensive Cost Analysis:** Conduct detailed cost assessments, factoring in data transfer fees, resource usage, and operational overhead.

- **Optimization Tools:** Use cost management tools like CloudHealth or Azure Cost Management to identify inefficiencies.

Organizational Resistance to Change and Skill Gaps

Transitioning to a hybrid cloud model often requires significant changes in organizational processes, tools, and culture. Resistance to change and skill gaps among staff can hinder adoption.

1. Resistance to Change

Challenge:
Teams accustomed to traditional IT practices may resist adopting new workflows or technologies associated with hybrid cloud.

Examples:

- Concerns over job security due to automation.

- Reluctance to learn new tools and platforms.

Solution:

- **Leadership Buy-In:** Gain support from leadership to champion hybrid cloud initiatives.

- **Clear Communication:** Explain the benefits of hybrid cloud, such as improved efficiency and career growth opportunities.

- **Pilot Programs:** Start with small-scale implementations to demonstrate success and build confidence.

---

2. Skill Gaps Among IT Staff

Challenge:
Hybrid cloud adoption requires expertise in cloud platforms, orchestration tools, and modern security practices, which many traditional IT teams may lack.

Examples:

- Limited knowledge of containerization tools like Docker and Kubernetes.

- Lack of experience with cloud-native security practices.

Solution:

- **Training and Upskilling:**
    - Offer training programs and certifications in relevant technologies (e.g., AWS, Azure, GCP).
    - Encourage participation in industry conferences and webinars.
- **Hire External Experts:**
    - Work with cloud consultants or hire experts to support complex projects.
- **Internal Mentorship Programs:** Pair experienced staff with less experienced team members to share knowledge.

---

3. Change Management

Challenge:
Rapid transitions to hybrid cloud environments can overwhelm teams if not managed carefully.

Examples:

- Confusion over new workflows.
- Increased stress due to tight deadlines.

Solution:

- **Phased Adoption:** Roll out hybrid cloud in stages, focusing on non-critical workloads first.

- **Change Agents:** Designate team members as change agents to guide others and address concerns.

- **Feedback Loops:** Create channels for employees to share feedback and suggest improvements.

Ensuring Seamless Collaboration Between Teams

Hybrid cloud adoption often involves multiple teams, including IT operations, development, security, and business units. Effective collaboration is crucial to prevent silos and ensure a unified approach.

1. Establishing Cross-Functional Teams

Definition:
Cross-functional teams bring together members

from different departments to collaborate on hybrid cloud projects.

Benefits:

- Improved communication and alignment.

- Faster decision-making.

- Holistic problem-solving.

Best Practices:

- Include representatives from IT, security, development, and business teams.

- Clearly define roles and responsibilities to avoid duplication of effort.

- Hold regular meetings to track progress and address issues.

---

2. Implementing DevOps Practices

Definition:
DevOps integrates development and operations teams to streamline workflows and enhance collaboration.

Benefits for Hybrid Cloud:

- Faster deployment of applications and updates.

- Improved communication between developers and IT teams.

- Enhanced scalability and reliability of hybrid cloud systems.

Key DevOps Tools:

- **CI/CD Pipelines:** Use Jenkins, GitLab CI/CD, or Azure DevOps to automate application delivery.

- **Collaboration Platforms:** Leverage tools like Slack, Microsoft Teams, or Atlassian Jira for communication and task management.

- **Infrastructure as Code (IaC):** Adopt Terraform or Ansible to standardize infrastructure provisioning.

---

3. Aligning Goals Across Teams

Challenge:
Different teams may have conflicting priorities, such as developers prioritizing speed while security teams focus on risk reduction.

Solution:

- **Unified Objectives:** Define shared goals, such as improving performance while maintaining security.

- **Metrics and KPIs:** Use metrics like time-to-deploy, security incidents, and resource utilization to track progress toward shared goals.

- **Regular Check-Ins:** Schedule cross-team meetings to address challenges and recalibrate objectives as needed.

---

4. Using Collaboration Tools

Definition:
Collaboration tools facilitate communication and project management across teams.

Examples:

- **Communication:** Slack, Microsoft Teams, Zoom.

- **Project Management:** Jira, Trello, Asana.

- **Documentation:** Confluence, Notion, or SharePoint for sharing knowledge and processes.

Benefits:

- Enhanced transparency and accountability.

- Faster resolution of issues through real-time collaboration.

Case Study: Overcoming Hybrid Cloud Adoption Challenges

Scenario:
A multinational retail company sought to adopt a hybrid cloud to improve scalability and enable real-time inventory management across its global operations.

Challenges:

- Legacy systems incompatible with cloud platforms.

- Resistance from IT staff unfamiliar with cloud technologies.

- Siloed teams causing delays in project execution.

Solutions:

1. **Integration Pitfalls Addressed:**
   - Used middleware to connect legacy systems to the cloud.
   - Migrated non-critical workloads first to minimize risks.

2. **Skill Gaps Overcome:**

- o Provided AWS and Azure training programs for IT staff.

- o Hired cloud architects to guide the initial implementation.

3. **Collaboration Enhanced:**

    - o Created cross-functional teams, including IT, development, and business leaders.

    - o Implemented DevOps practices to accelerate application deployment.

Outcome:

- Reduced inventory processing time by 50%.

- Enabled seamless collaboration between teams.

- Improved employee confidence in using hybrid cloud technologies.

Addressing the challenges of hybrid cloud adoption requires a multifaceted approach that tackles technical, organizational, and cultural barriers. By avoiding integration pitfalls, addressing resistance and skill gaps, and fostering collaboration between teams, organizations can unlock the full potential of hybrid cloud environments.

In the next chapter, we will explore regulatory and compliance considerations in hybrid cloud solutions, focusing on how organizations can meet industry standards while leveraging hybrid cloud benefits.

Chapter 16: Regulatory and Compliance Considerations

Hybrid cloud environments offer flexibility, scalability, and cost efficiency, but they also present unique regulatory and compliance challenges. Organizations must ensure that their hybrid cloud solutions adhere to industry-specific requirements, global data protection laws, and governance standards. This chapter explores key compliance requirements, strategies for adhering to regulations like GDPR and HIPAA, and best practices for auditing and reporting in hybrid environments.

Industry-Specific Compliance Requirements

Different industries operate under unique regulatory frameworks designed to ensure data security, privacy, and integrity. Understanding these requirements is critical for organizations using hybrid cloud environments.

---

1. Financial Services

The financial sector is heavily regulated to protect sensitive customer information, ensure fair practices, and mitigate risks.

Key Regulations:

- **PCI DSS (Payment Card Industry Data Security Standard):** Ensures the security of credit card transactions.

- **SOX (Sarbanes-Oxley Act):** Governs financial reporting and auditing.

- **FFIEC (Federal Financial Institutions Examination Council):** Provides standards for IT and cybersecurity in financial institutions.

Compliance Challenges in Hybrid Cloud:

- Storing and processing sensitive financial data across multiple environments.

- Ensuring data encryption during transfer and at rest.

- Maintaining consistent auditing and reporting practices.

Best Practices:

- Use encryption and tokenization to secure payment data in cloud and on-premises systems.

- Implement continuous monitoring to detect and respond to anomalies.

- Partner with cloud providers certified for PCI DSS and other financial standards.

---

2. Healthcare

Healthcare organizations handle highly sensitive patient data and are subject to stringent privacy and security requirements.

Key Regulations:

- **HIPAA (Health Insurance Portability and Accountability Act):** Governs the protection of patient health information (PHI) in the U.S.

- **HITECH (Health Information Technology for Economic and Clinical Health Act):** Strengthens HIPAA's requirements for electronic health records.

- **GDPR (General Data Protection Regulation):** Impacts healthcare providers handling EU citizens' data.

Compliance Challenges in Hybrid Cloud:

- Safeguarding PHI in both cloud and on-premises systems.

- Ensuring data is not stored or processed outside permitted jurisdictions.

- Maintaining access controls to prevent unauthorized data access.

Best Practices:

- Store sensitive PHI on-premises and use the cloud for non-sensitive workloads, such as analytics.

- Encrypt data in transit and at rest to meet HIPAA requirements.

- Choose cloud providers offering Business Associate Agreements (BAAs) for HIPAA compliance.

---

3. Retail and E-Commerce

Retailers and e-commerce companies handle significant volumes of customer data, making compliance with data privacy laws and payment standards critical.

Key Regulations:

- **PCI DSS:** Ensures secure payment processing.

- **CCPA (California Consumer Privacy Act):** Governs consumer data privacy in California.

- **GDPR:** Protects personal data of EU customers.

Compliance Challenges in Hybrid Cloud:

- Managing cross-border data transfers.

- Protecting customer data from breaches or unauthorized access.

- Ensuring secure payment processing in hybrid environments.

Best Practices:

- Implement robust encryption protocols for payment transactions.

- Use data localization to meet regional requirements.

- Regularly audit access controls to prevent data breaches.

4. Government and Defense

Government agencies handle sensitive and classified information, requiring stringent compliance with security and privacy standards.

Key Regulations:

- **FedRAMP (Federal Risk and Authorization Management Program):** Ensures secure cloud usage by U.S. federal agencies.

- **CJIS (Criminal Justice Information Services):** Protects criminal justice data in the U.S.

- **NIST (National Institute of Standards and Technology) Standards:** Provides cybersecurity frameworks.

Compliance Challenges in Hybrid Cloud:

- Storing classified data in highly secure environments.

- Ensuring data integrity and availability during disasters or cyberattacks.

- Adhering to government-specific cloud certifications.

Best Practices:

- Use government-certified cloud providers like AWS GovCloud or Azure Government.

- Implement multi-factor authentication (MFA) for secure access.

- Regularly test disaster recovery plans to meet continuity requirements.

Adhering to GDPR, HIPAA, and Other Standards

Global and regional data protection regulations such as GDPR and HIPAA impose strict rules on how organizations handle personal data. Adhering to these standards is critical for hybrid cloud environments.

---

1. General Data Protection Regulation (GDPR)

Scope:
Applies to organizations processing personal data of EU citizens, regardless of location.

Key Requirements:

- Obtain explicit consent for data collection and processing.

- Provide data subjects with the right to access, correct, and delete their data.

- Notify authorities and affected individuals of data breaches within 72 hours.

Challenges in Hybrid Cloud:

- Ensuring data sovereignty and avoiding unauthorized cross-border transfers.
- Maintaining records of data processing activities across environments.

Best Practices:

- Use data localization tools to store EU data within the region.
- Implement encryption and pseudonymization to protect personal data.
- Partner with GDPR-compliant cloud providers.

---

2. Health Insurance Portability and Accountability Act (HIPAA)

Scope:
Regulates the use, storage, and transmission of PHI in the U.S.

Key Requirements:

- Ensure data confidentiality, integrity, and availability.

- Implement administrative, physical, and technical safeguards for PHI.

- Execute Business Associate Agreements (BAAs) with cloud providers handling PHI.

Challenges in Hybrid Cloud:

- Maintaining strict access controls across environments.

- Ensuring secure data backups and disaster recovery.

Best Practices:

- Use IAM solutions to enforce role-based access to PHI.

- Encrypt all data at rest and in transit.

- Conduct regular risk assessments to identify vulnerabilities.

---

3. Payment Card Industry Data Security Standard (PCI DSS)

Scope:
Applies to organizations handling credit card transactions.

Key Requirements:

- Protect cardholder data using encryption and tokenization.

- Regularly test security systems and processes.

- Maintain a secure network with firewalls and access controls.

Challenges in Hybrid Cloud:

- Securing payment data during cross-environment transfers.

- Managing compliance across multi-cloud and on-premises systems.

Best Practices:

- Use dedicated private networks for payment processing.

- Perform regular penetration testing to identify and mitigate risks.

- Partner with PCI DSS-compliant cloud providers.

Auditing and Reporting in Hybrid Environments

Auditing and reporting are critical for ensuring compliance and maintaining transparency in hybrid cloud environments.

---

1. Key Audit Areas

a. Access Controls:

- Ensure only authorized users can access sensitive data.

- Maintain logs of access and modifications for accountability.

b. Data Transfers:

- Track data movement between on-premises and cloud systems to detect unauthorized transfers.

c. Security Measures:

- Verify the implementation of encryption, firewalls, and intrusion detection systems.

---

2. Tools for Auditing and Reporting

a. Cloud-Native Tools:

- **AWS CloudTrail:** Tracks user activity and API usage for auditing purposes.

- **Azure Security Center:** Provides compliance reports and risk assessments.

- **Google Cloud Audit Logs:** Captures logs of administrative and data access activities.

b. Third-Party Tools:

- **Splunk:** Centralizes logs from hybrid environments for compliance reporting.

- **ServiceNow:** Automates auditing workflows and tracks compliance metrics.

- **Qualys:** Conducts security and compliance audits across hybrid systems.

---

3. Best Practices for Auditing

a. Automate Reporting:

- Use tools to automate compliance reporting, reducing manual effort and ensuring accuracy.

b. Establish Clear Policies:

- Define policies for log retention, data access, and incident response.

c. Regular Audits:

- Schedule periodic audits to verify compliance and address gaps proactively.

d. Cross-Environment Visibility:

- Ensure auditing tools can capture data from both on-premises and cloud systems for a unified view.

Case Study: Hybrid Cloud Compliance Success

Scenario:
A global pharmaceutical company adopted a hybrid cloud strategy to support R&D and comply with stringent regulations like GDPR and HIPAA.

Challenges:

- Managing sensitive patient data across regions.

- Ensuring data sovereignty for EU operations.

- Maintaining compliance with HIPAA for U.S.-based operations.

Solution:

1. **Data Localization:** Used cloud regions in the EU and U.S. to store sensitive data locally.

2. **Compliance Tools:** Leveraged AWS Artifact for GDPR compliance and Azure Security Center for HIPAA adherence.

3. **Auditing:** Deployed Splunk to centralize logs and generate compliance reports.

Outcome:

- Achieved full compliance with GDPR and HIPAA.

- Streamlined R&D operations with secure data sharing.

- Reduced compliance auditing time by 40% through automation.

Navigating regulatory and compliance requirements in hybrid cloud environments requires a deep understanding of industry-specific standards, robust security practices, and effective auditing tools. By adopting best practices and leveraging advanced compliance technologies, organizations can achieve secure, compliant, and efficient hybrid cloud operations.

In the next chapter, we will explore emerging trends in hybrid cloud computing, discussing how new technologies and approaches are shaping the future of hybrid IT environments.

Chapter 17: Future Trends in Hybrid Cloud Technology

As technology continues to evolve, hybrid cloud environments are at the forefront of innovation, enabling organizations to achieve new levels of scalability, efficiency, and intelligence. Emerging trends such as AI and machine learning, edge computing, and quantum computing are reshaping how hybrid clouds are designed, deployed, and managed. This chapter delves into these transformative trends, examining their role in hybrid cloud management and their potential to redefine the future of IT.

AI and Machine Learning in Hybrid Cloud Management

Artificial Intelligence (AI) and Machine Learning (ML) are revolutionizing hybrid cloud management by automating complex tasks, optimizing resource allocation, and enhancing security.

1. Enhancing Cloud Operations with AI

Definition:
AI-driven operations (AIOps) leverage machine learning and big data analytics to automate and optimize IT operations in hybrid cloud environments.

Applications in Hybrid Cloud:

- **Resource Optimization:** AI analyzes usage patterns to recommend optimal resource allocation, reducing costs and preventing overprovisioning.

- **Predictive Maintenance:** Machine learning models predict potential hardware or software failures, enabling proactive interventions.

- **Capacity Planning:** AI forecasts future demand, ensuring resources are available without overspending.

Examples:

- AWS uses AI in its Compute Optimizer to suggest optimal instance types for workloads.

- Microsoft Azure's AI tools monitor performance and predict future capacity needs.

---

2. Automating Security with AI

Role of AI in Hybrid Cloud Security:

- **Threat Detection:** AI identifies unusual behavior or anomalies that could indicate security breaches.

- **Incident Response:** Automated responses, such as isolating compromised resources or applying patches, reduce response times.

- **Access Management:** AI enforces role-based access controls and detects unauthorized access attempts.

Tools for AI-Driven Security:

- **IBM Watson AIOps:** Uses AI to detect, diagnose, and respond to incidents.

- **Google Cloud Security AI:** Enhances threat intelligence and automates security workflows.

---

3. Improving Application Performance with ML

Applications of ML:

- **Dynamic Load Balancing:** Machine learning algorithms distribute traffic intelligently across resources to maintain optimal performance.

- **Anomaly Detection:** ML models detect deviations in performance metrics, helping IT teams resolve issues before users are affected.

- **DevOps Integration:** ML-powered CI/CD pipelines optimize application testing and deployment processes.

Examples:

- Netflix uses AI to predict demand and scale resources dynamically, ensuring uninterrupted streaming.

- A retail company uses ML to analyze customer traffic patterns, scaling hybrid cloud resources during sales events.

Edge Computing and Its Role in Hybrid Environments

Edge computing is redefining hybrid cloud architecture by bringing processing closer to where data is generated. This trend enhances latency-sensitive applications, supports IoT, and reduces bandwidth costs.

---

1. What Is Edge Computing?

Definition:
Edge computing refers to processing data at or near the data source (e.g., IoT devices, edge servers) rather than sending it to centralized cloud servers.

Benefits in Hybrid Cloud:

- **Reduced Latency:** Processes time-sensitive data locally, enabling real-time decision-making.

- **Bandwidth Efficiency:** Minimizes data transfers to the cloud, lowering costs.

- **Enhanced Resilience:** Localized processing ensures operations continue even if cloud connectivity is disrupted.

---

2. Use Cases of Edge Computing in Hybrid Cloud

a. IoT and Smart Devices:

- Edge computing processes data from IoT sensors in real time, with critical insights stored locally and long-term data sent to the cloud.

- Example: A manufacturing plant uses edge computing to monitor equipment performance and prevent downtime.

b. Autonomous Vehicles:

- Self-driving cars process sensor data locally for immediate decision-making while uploading aggregated data to the cloud for analysis.

c. Retail:

- Edge servers process in-store analytics, such as customer foot traffic and inventory tracking, with cloud resources handling predictive analytics and reporting.

d. Healthcare:

- Medical devices use edge computing for real-time monitoring and diagnostics, ensuring quick responses in critical situations.

3. Integration of Edge Computing with Hybrid Cloud

Challenges:

- **Data Synchronization:** Ensuring consistency between edge devices and central cloud systems.

- **Security:** Protecting edge devices from unauthorized access and attacks.

- **Scalability:** Managing a large network of distributed edge devices efficiently.

Solutions:

- **Orchestration Tools:** Kubernetes-based solutions like K3s manage containerized workloads at the edge.

- **Edge-Specific Platforms:** AWS IoT Greengrass, Azure IoT Edge, and Google Distributed Cloud support hybrid edge computing.

- **Security Practices:** Implement device-level encryption and AI-driven anomaly detection to secure edge deployments.

The Impact of Emerging Technologies like Quantum Computing

Quantum computing, though still in its early stages, has the potential to revolutionize hybrid cloud environments by solving problems that are intractable for classical computers.

1. What Is Quantum Computing?

Definition:
Quantum computing leverages quantum bits (qubits) to perform computations that exploit the principles of superposition, entanglement, and quantum interference.

Key Features:

- **Exponential Speedup:** Solves complex problems much faster than traditional systems.

- **Parallelism:** Processes multiple possibilities simultaneously.

2. Potential Applications in Hybrid Cloud

a. Cryptography and Security:

- Quantum computers can crack traditional encryption methods, necessitating quantum-safe cryptography. Hybrid cloud environments will integrate quantum cryptography to secure sensitive data.

b. Optimization Problems:

- Quantum algorithms can optimize resource allocation, traffic routing, and supply chain logistics in hybrid cloud environments.

c. Drug Discovery and Healthcare:

- Hybrid clouds incorporating quantum computing can simulate molecular interactions for faster drug development.

d. AI and Machine Learning:

- Quantum computing accelerates the training of complex AI models, enhancing analytics and decision-making in hybrid clouds.

3. Challenges of Quantum Integration in Hybrid Cloud

a. Cost and Accessibility:

- Quantum hardware is expensive and not yet widely available.

- Cloud-based quantum services, like IBM Quantum and AWS Braket, offer initial access.

b. Interoperability:

- Integrating quantum systems with classical cloud infrastructure is technically complex.

c. Skills Gap:

- Specialized knowledge is required to develop and implement quantum algorithms.

---

4. Future of Quantum Computing in Hybrid Cloud

Short-Term Impact:

- Quantum as a Service (QaaS) offerings will enable organizations to experiment with quantum computing without owning hardware.

Long-Term Impact:

- Hybrid cloud environments will incorporate quantum co-processors to tackle specific tasks, while classical systems handle routine workloads.

Synergy of Emerging Technologies

The convergence of AI, edge computing, and quantum computing is shaping the future of hybrid cloud environments.

---

1. AI-Driven Edge Computing

- AI models deployed at the edge enhance decision-making in real-time, supporting applications like predictive maintenance and personalized retail experiences.

2. Quantum-Enhanced AI

- Quantum computing accelerates AI model training, enabling faster deployment of intelligent systems in hybrid clouds.

3. Hybrid Edge-Quantum Integration

- Hybrid architectures will combine edge computing's low latency with quantum computing's computational power for breakthrough innovations.

Case Study: Emerging Technologies in Hybrid Cloud

Scenario:
A global logistics company adopted a hybrid cloud strategy integrating AI, edge computing, and quantum computing to optimize operations.

Challenges:

- Real-time tracking of shipments across diverse geographies.

- Optimizing delivery routes to reduce fuel costs.

- Securing sensitive customer data during transit.

Solution:

1. **AI-Driven Insights:**
   - Deployed AI models on edge devices to analyze traffic and weather patterns in real time.

- o Used cloud-based AI for predictive analytics on supply chain trends.

2. **Edge Computing for Real-Time Tracking:**

- o Edge servers processed data from IoT sensors on vehicles, reducing latency and enabling real-time visibility.

3. **Quantum Computing for Optimization:**

- o Leveraged a cloud-based quantum platform to optimize delivery routes and minimize delays.

Outcome:

- Reduced fuel costs by 15% through optimized routes.

- Achieved real-time shipment tracking with 99% accuracy.

- Strengthened customer trust with end-to-end data security.

The future of hybrid cloud technology is being shaped by groundbreaking advancements in AI, edge computing, and quantum computing. These technologies are driving innovation, enhancing efficiency, and solving previously intractable problems. As hybrid cloud environments evolve, organizations must embrace these trends to remain competitive and unlock new possibilities.

Chapter 18: Hands-On Tutorials and Projects

This chapter provides a practical guide to implementing hybrid cloud solutions through hands-on tutorials and projects. By setting up a hybrid cloud demo environment, migrating a sample application, and building a hybrid CI/CD pipeline, you'll gain the skills needed to design and deploy robust hybrid cloud architectures.

Tutorial 1: Setting Up a Hybrid Cloud Demo Environment

This tutorial demonstrates how to set up a hybrid cloud environment connecting an on-premises infrastructure with a public cloud provider. We'll use **AWS**, a popular public cloud platform, and a **local virtual machine (VM)** to simulate on-premises resources.

1. Prerequisites

- An **AWS account** with administrative privileges.

- A local machine with **VirtualBox** or a similar hypervisor installed.

- Basic knowledge of networking and cloud services.

---

2. Steps to Set Up the Environment

Step 1: Launch a Local Virtual Machine

1. Install VirtualBox on your local machine.

2. Create a new VM:

   - Select an operating system (e.g., Ubuntu Server).

   - Allocate resources (2 CPUs, 4 GB RAM, 20 GB disk).

3. Start the VM and install the necessary software (e.g., Docker, Apache, or MySQL).

Step 2: Create a VPC in AWS

1. Log in to the AWS Management Console.

2. Navigate to **VPC (Virtual Private Cloud)** and create a new VPC.

3. Set up subnets for public and private resources:

   o Public subnet: For resources accessible from the internet.

   o Private subnet: For backend resources (e.g., databases).

4. Configure a security group to allow SSH, HTTP, and HTTPS traffic.

Step 3: Establish Connectivity Between On-Premises and AWS

1. Use **AWS Site-to-Site VPN** to connect the on-premises VM and the AWS VPC:

   o Set up a VPN gateway in AWS.

   o Configure a virtual private gateway.

   o Use your local VM's public IP to establish the VPN connection.

2. Verify connectivity by pinging AWS resources from the local VM.

Step 4: Deploy Resources in AWS

1. Launch an EC2 instance in the public subnet.

2. Install a web server (e.g., Apache) on the instance.

3. Configure DNS settings for the instance using AWS Route 53.

Validation:

- Test connectivity by accessing the EC2 instance from your on-premises VM.

- Verify that traffic flows seamlessly between on-premises and cloud environments.

Tutorial 2: Migrating a Sample Application to a Hybrid Cloud Architecture

In this tutorial, we will migrate a simple **LAMP stack (Linux, Apache, MySQL, PHP)** application to a hybrid cloud setup. The database will remain on-premises, while the web server will run on a cloud platform.

1. Prerequisites

- A running LAMP stack application on an on-premises VM.

- Access to an AWS account for deploying cloud resources.

2. Steps for Migration

Step 1: Prepare the On-Premises Database

1. Ensure the MySQL database is running on your local VM.

2. Open the MySQL configuration file (/etc/mysql/mysql.conf.d/mysqld.cnf) and allow remote access:

css

bind-address = 0.0.0.0

3. Create a user with remote access permissions:

sql

```
CREATE USER 'remote_user'@'%' IDENTIFIED BY 'password';
GRANT ALL PRIVILEGES ON *.* TO 'remote_user'@'%';
FLUSH PRIVILEGES;
```

4. Configure the firewall to allow traffic on the MySQL port (default: 3306).

Step 2: Deploy the Web Server on AWS

1. Launch an EC2 instance in your AWS account.

2. Install Apache and PHP:

bash

```
sudo apt update

sudo apt install apache2 php libapache2-mod-php
-y
```

3. Copy your application files from the on-premises VM to the EC2 instance using scp.

Step 3: Connect the Web Server to the On-Premises Database

1. Update the application's database configuration file to use the on-premises MySQL server's IP address.

2. Test the connection by running the application on the EC2 instance.

Step 4: Validate and Optimize

1. Test the application from an external browser.

2. Use AWS CloudWatch to monitor the performance of the EC2 instance.

Advanced Step:

- Configure a load balancer in AWS to handle traffic to the web server.

- Set up an RDS instance in AWS as a backup database, replicating data from the on-premises MySQL server.

Tutorial 3: Building and Deploying a Hybrid CI/CD Pipeline

This tutorial guides you through creating a CI/CD pipeline that spans on-premises and cloud resources. The pipeline will build and deploy a containerized application.

1. Prerequisites

- **GitHub** account to host the application's source code.

- **Docker** installed on the on-premises VM.

- An AWS account with access to **Elastic Container Service (ECS)**.

2. Steps to Build the Pipeline

Step 1: Containerize the Application

1. Write a Dockerfile for your application. For example:

dockerfile

FROM php:7.4-apache

COPY . /var/www/html/

EXPOSE 80

2. Build the Docker image on the on-premises VM:

bash

docker build -t my-app:latest .

3. Test the container locally to ensure it runs correctly.

Step 2: Push the Image to a Cloud Repository

1. Create an **Amazon Elastic Container Registry (ECR)** repository in AWS.

2. Authenticate Docker with the ECR:

bash

```
aws ecr get-login-password --region <region> |
docker login --username AWS --password-stdin
<account_id>.dkr.ecr.<region>.amazonaws.com
```

3. Push the Docker image to the ECR:

bash

```
docker tag my-app:latest
<account_id>.dkr.ecr.<region>.amazonaws.com/my-app:latest
docker push
<account_id>.dkr.ecr.<region>.amazonaws.com/my-app:latest
```

Step 3: Set Up the CI/CD Pipeline

1. Create a **GitHub Actions** workflow:

   o Add a .github/workflows/deploy.yml
     file to your repository:

yaml

```
name: CI/CD Pipeline
```

```yaml
on:
  push:
    branches:
      - main

jobs:
  build:
    runs-on: ubuntu-latest

    steps:
      - name: Checkout Code
        uses: actions/checkout@v2

      - name: Build Docker Image
        run: docker build -t my-app:latest .

      - name: Push to ECR
        env:
          AWS_REGION: <region>
```

```
AWS_ACCESS_KEY_ID: ${{
secrets.AWS_ACCESS_KEY_ID }}

AWS_SECRET_ACCESS_KEY: ${{
secrets.AWS_SECRET_ACCESS_KEY }}

run: |

aws ecr get-login-password --region
$AWS_REGION | docker login --username AWS --
password-stdin
<account_id>.dkr.ecr.$AWS_REGION.amazonaws.c
om

docker tag my-app:latest
<account_id>.dkr.ecr.$AWS_REGION.amazonaws.c
om/my-app:latest

docker push
<account_id>.dkr.ecr.$AWS_REGION.amazonaws.c
om/my-app:latest
```

2. Add AWS credentials to your GitHub repository's secrets.

Step 4: Deploy the Application to AWS ECS

1. Create an ECS cluster and define a task using the pushed Docker image.

2. Deploy the task to the ECS cluster.

3. Use AWS Fargate or EC2 instances for running the containers.

Validation:

- Push a code change to the GitHub repository and confirm that the pipeline builds and deploys the updated image to ECS.

These hands-on tutorials provide a practical foundation for implementing hybrid cloud solutions, from setting up a demo environment to migrating applications and deploying CI/CD pipelines. By mastering these projects, you'll gain valuable experience in hybrid cloud architecture and management, preparing you for real-world challenges and innovations.

Chapter 19: Troubleshooting Hybrid Cloud Issues

Managing a hybrid cloud environment comes with its share of complexities. From connectivity glitches to performance bottlenecks, identifying and resolving issues is critical to maintaining operational efficiency. This chapter provides a comprehensive guide to troubleshooting hybrid cloud issues by addressing common problems, outlining best practices for debugging, and explaining how to leverage community and vendor support effectively.

Identifying Common Problems and Root Causes

Hybrid cloud environments combine on-premises and cloud systems, creating a broad range of potential issues that may arise due to network configurations, resource mismatches, or application compatibility.

1. Network Connectivity Issues

Symptoms:

- Inability to access cloud resources from on-premises systems.
- Intermittent connectivity between hybrid cloud components.
- High latency affecting application performance.

Root Causes:

- Misconfigured VPNs or direct connections.
- Firewall rules blocking required ports or IP ranges.
- Network address translation (NAT) conflicts or overlapping IP ranges.

Troubleshooting Steps:

1. Verify the status of VPN or direct connections.
2. Use tools like **ping, traceroute**, or **nslookup** to identify network bottlenecks.
3. Check firewall and security group rules to ensure they allow necessary traffic.

4. Resolve overlapping IP range conflicts by reconfiguring subnets.

---

2. Performance Degradation

Symptoms:

- Slower application response times.

- High resource utilization on cloud or on-premises systems.

- Delays in processing or transferring data.

Root Causes:

- Overprovisioned or underprovisioned resources.

- Insufficient bandwidth for data transfers.

- Latency introduced by long network paths or inefficient routing.

Troubleshooting Steps:

1. Use monitoring tools like **AWS CloudWatch**, **Azure Monitor**, or **Datadog** to identify resource bottlenecks.

2. Test network performance with tools like **iperf** or **Wireshark**.

3. Optimize workload placement to reduce data transfer overhead.

---

3. Application Compatibility Issues

Symptoms:

- Applications fail to run after migration to the cloud.
- Errors related to missing dependencies or unsupported configurations.

Root Causes:

- Legacy applications incompatible with cloud environments.
- Differences in operating systems or middleware versions.
- Missing or misconfigured libraries and dependencies.

Troubleshooting Steps:

1. Test applications in a staging environment before migration.
2. Use containerization tools like Docker to package dependencies consistently.
3. Update application code or configurations to support hybrid cloud deployment.

4. Security Breaches or Misconfigurations

Symptoms:

- Unauthorized access to sensitive data or systems.
- Security alerts triggered by anomalous activities.
- Inconsistent application of security policies across environments.

Root Causes:

- Misconfigured IAM policies or firewall rules.
- Unencrypted data in transit or at rest.
- Failure to apply security patches promptly.

Troubleshooting Steps:

1. Audit security policies using tools like **AWS IAM Access Analyzer** or **Azure Security Center**.
2. Encrypt data using TLS/SSL for transit and AES-256 for storage.
3. Regularly update and patch software and systems.

Best Practices for Debugging and Issue Resolution

Effective debugging and resolution require a structured approach, clear processes, and the right tools.

1. Establish a Troubleshooting Framework

a. Define the Problem:

- Collect logs, error messages, and user reports to understand the issue clearly.

b. Isolate the Issue:

- Narrow down potential causes by systematically testing different components.

c. Identify Root Causes:

- Use tools and diagnostic methods to pinpoint the root cause of the problem.

d. Implement Solutions:

- Apply fixes incrementally and test each change to avoid unintended side effects.

2. Use Diagnostic and Monitoring Tools

a. Monitoring Platforms:

- **AWS CloudWatch:** Monitor resource usage, application performance, and system logs.

- **Azure Monitor:** Provides insights into hybrid workloads and connected environments.

- **Google Cloud Operations Suite:** Tracks metrics, traces, and logs for GCP environments.

b. Network Analysis Tools:

- **Wireshark:** Capture and analyze network traffic to identify bottlenecks.

- **Traceroute:** Trace network paths to diagnose latency and connectivity issues.

c. Log Aggregation Tools:

- **Splunk:** Centralizes and analyzes logs from hybrid environments.

- **Elastic Stack (ELK):** Collects, searches, and visualizes log data.

3. Implement Proactive Monitoring

a. Set Up Alerts:

- Configure thresholds for critical metrics like CPU usage, latency, or error rates.

- Use automated alerts to detect and respond to issues before they impact users.

b. Automate Incident Response:

- Use tools like AWS Lambda or Azure Logic Apps to automate responses to predefined triggers.

- Example: Automatically scaling resources during high traffic.

c. Establish a Baseline:

- Monitor normal behavior to detect anomalies effectively.

---

4. Perform Regular Maintenance and Updates

a. Update Configurations:

- Periodically review and update security groups, IAM policies, and network settings.

b. Patch Management:

- Automate patch deployment using tools like AWS Systems Manager or Microsoft Endpoint Manager.

c. Backup and Test Recovery Plans:

- Ensure data backups are up to date and perform regular disaster recovery tests.

5. Build a Knowledge Base

- Document common issues, resolutions, and lessons learned.

- Share troubleshooting guides and runbooks with relevant teams to streamline issue resolution.

Leveraging Community and Vendor Support

When internal resources and expertise fall short, the hybrid cloud ecosystem offers abundant support through vendor services, community forums, and professional consultants.

1. Vendor Support Services

a. AWS Support:

- **Basic Tier:** Limited to account and billing support.

- **Developer Tier:** Provides technical support and best practices guidance.

- **Enterprise Tier:** Includes dedicated Technical Account Managers (TAMs) and 24/7 support.

b. Microsoft Azure Support:

- Offers support plans ranging from Developer to Premier tiers.

- Includes features like proactive monitoring, escalation management, and advisory services.

c. Google Cloud Support:

- Support tiers include Basic, Development, Production, and Premium levels.

- Premium support offers account management and technical support for complex issues.

2. Community Forums and Resources

a. Online Forums:

- **Stack Overflow:** Active discussions on troubleshooting coding and system issues.

- **Reddit (r/cloudcomputing):** Insights and experiences shared by IT professionals.

b. Vendor Communities:

- AWS, Azure, and Google Cloud maintain active forums and community spaces for knowledge sharing.

c. Documentation and Tutorials:

- Official documentation often contains detailed troubleshooting steps.

---

3. Third-Party Support

a. Managed Service Providers (MSPs):

- MSPs offer end-to-end management of hybrid cloud environments, including troubleshooting and optimization.

b. Consultants and Specialists:

- Engage certified consultants for expertise in hybrid cloud deployment and debugging.

- Example: AWS Certified Solutions Architects or Azure Experts.

4. Open-Source Communities

a. GitHub Repositories:

- Explore repositories for hybrid cloud tools, scripts, and troubleshooting utilities.

b. Open-Source Tools Support:

- Use community channels for tools like Kubernetes, Terraform, or Prometheus to resolve issues.

Case Study: Resolving a Hybrid Cloud Connectivity Issue

Scenario:

A global retail company experienced intermittent connectivity between its on-premises database and cloud-hosted e-commerce platform, leading to frequent checkout errors during peak traffic.

Challenges:

- High latency and packet loss during data synchronization.

- Errors in API communication between systems.

Steps to Resolution:

1. **Diagnosing the Issue:**

   - Used Wireshark to analyze network traffic and identify packet loss at specific intervals.

   - Verified API logs to uncover configuration mismatches.

2. **Implementing Fixes:**

   - Reconfigured the VPN to resolve latency issues.

   - Updated API settings to improve compatibility between systems.

3. **Validating the Fix:**

   - Monitored system performance during a simulated traffic spike to confirm stability.

Outcome:

- Reduced checkout errors by 90%.

- Improved data transfer speeds by 30%, enhancing user experience.

Troubleshooting hybrid cloud issues requires a structured approach, a deep understanding of potential problem areas, and effective use of tools and support resources. By identifying root causes, implementing best practices, and leveraging community and vendor assistance, organizations can maintain robust, efficient, and secure hybrid cloud operations.

In the next chapter, we will conclude this guide by summarizing the key takeaways from the book and outlining actionable steps for continued success in hybrid cloud implementation and management.

Chapter 20: Conclusion and Next Steps

Hybrid cloud computing has transformed how organizations approach IT infrastructure, enabling unparalleled flexibility, scalability, and efficiency. This guide has provided a comprehensive exploration of hybrid cloud technologies, from foundational concepts to advanced strategies and hands-on tutorials. In this concluding chapter, we will summarize the key takeaways, outline steps for building a future-ready hybrid cloud strategy, and provide resources for continuous learning and growth.

Key Takeaways from the Guide

The journey through hybrid cloud technology covered various topics that together form a holistic understanding of this transformative approach.

1. The Basics of Hybrid Cloud

- A **hybrid cloud** combines on-premises infrastructure with public and private cloud resources, offering the best of both worlds: control and scalability.

- Common drivers for hybrid cloud adoption include cost optimization, enhanced agility, and compliance requirements.

2. Core Components of a Hybrid Cloud Environment

- Hybrid cloud architectures rely on **secure connectivity**, **data management**, and **integration tools** to ensure seamless communication between systems.

- Networking solutions like **VPNs, direct connections**, and **SD-WANs** are critical for maintaining performance and reliability.

3. Benefits and Challenges

- **Benefits:** Improved operational efficiency, cost savings, regulatory compliance, and scalability.

- **Challenges:** Complex integration, security vulnerabilities, and organizational resistance to change.

---

4. Strategies and Best Practices

- **Workload Distribution:** Identify which workloads are best suited for the cloud versus on-premises.

- **Security:** Employ robust access controls, encryption, and monitoring to safeguard data.

- **Cost Management:** Use tools and strategies like **Infrastructure as Code (IaC)** and **multi-cloud approaches** to optimize spending.

---

5. Hands-On Learning

Practical tutorials demonstrated how to:

- Set up a hybrid cloud environment.

- Migrate applications.

- Build and deploy hybrid CI/CD pipelines.

Building a Hybrid Cloud Strategy for the Future

As hybrid cloud technology evolves, organizations must adopt forward-thinking strategies to remain competitive and adaptive to change.

---

1. Assessing Your Current State

a. Inventory Resources:

- Catalog existing on-premises infrastructure and cloud deployments.

- Identify underutilized or legacy resources that can be optimized or retired.

b. Evaluate Workload Suitability:

- Determine which workloads are best suited for on-premises, cloud, or hybrid environments.

- Use tools like **Azure Migrate** or **AWS Migration Evaluator** for data-driven assessments.

c. Understand Business Objectives:

- Align hybrid cloud goals with business priorities, such as cost reduction, improved agility, or global expansion.

2. Designing a Future-Ready Architecture

a. Embrace Modular Design:

- Build a hybrid cloud architecture with flexibility in mind, using microservices and containerization.

b. Prioritize Interoperability:

- Ensure your systems, tools, and applications can work seamlessly across cloud providers.

- Use open-source technologies like **Kubernetes** to avoid vendor lock-in.

c. Leverage Emerging Technologies:

- Integrate **AI**, **edge computing**, and **quantum computing** as they become more accessible to stay ahead of industry trends.

3. Implementing Governance and Security

a. Establish Clear Policies:

- Define rules for data handling, access controls, and compliance across hybrid environments.

b. Automate Compliance:

- Use tools like **AWS Config, Azure Policy,** or **Google Cloud Security Command Center** to enforce compliance in real-time.

c. Foster a Culture of Security:

- Train employees on best practices and involve all teams in maintaining security standards.

---

4. Continuous Monitoring and Optimization

a. Proactive Monitoring:

- Deploy monitoring tools like **Datadog, Splunk,** or **CloudWatch** to track performance and detect anomalies.

b. Optimize Costs:

- Regularly review cloud expenditures, adjust resource allocations, and leverage cost-saving strategies like reserved instances.

c. Periodic Audits:

- Perform audits to ensure architecture aligns with business goals and to identify areas for improvement.

---

5. Fostering Organizational Change

a. Build Cross-Functional Teams:

- Encourage collaboration between IT, security, and business units to maximize the potential of hybrid cloud.

b. Provide Training:

- Upskill employees in cloud-native technologies, security, and automation tools.

- Offer certifications from major cloud providers (e.g., AWS, Azure, GCP).

c. Promote a Growth Mindset:

- Encourage experimentation and innovation while learning from failures.

Resources for Continuous Learning and Growth

Hybrid cloud technology is constantly evolving. Staying informed and skilled requires commitment to ongoing education and engagement with the tech community.

1. Online Learning Platforms

a. Cloud Provider Resources:

- **AWS Training and Certification:** Courses on foundational to advanced topics.

- **Microsoft Learn (Azure):** Free learning paths for Azure technologies.

- **Google Cloud Skills Boost:** Training on GCP services and solutions.

b. MOOCs:

- Platforms like **Coursera, edX**, and **Udemy** offer courses on hybrid cloud architecture, DevOps, and related fields.

c. YouTube Channels:

- **AWS Online Tech Talks**

- **Microsoft Azure Tech Community**

- **Google Cloud Platform Channel**

---

2. Certifications

Pursue certifications to validate your expertise:

- **AWS Certified Solutions Architect – Professional**

- **Microsoft Certified: Azure Solutions Architect Expert**

- **Google Cloud Professional Cloud Architect**

- **Certified Kubernetes Administrator (CKA)**

---

3. Industry Events and Webinars

- Attend conferences like **AWS re:Invent, Microsoft Ignite,** and **Google Cloud Next** to learn about the latest advancements.

- Join webinars hosted by vendors or industry leaders for hands-on demos and insights.

---

4. Technical Communities and Forums

a. Forums:

- **Stack Overflow:** Problem-solving for developers.

- **Reddit (r/cloudcomputing):** Discuss hybrid cloud trends and best practices.

b. Communities:

- **Cloud Native Computing Foundation (CNCF):** Focus on Kubernetes and cloud-native technologies.

- **Hybrid Cloud User Groups:** Join local or virtual meetups to connect with peers.

---

5. Books and Publications

- **"Hybrid Cloud for Dummies"** by Judith Hurwitz: A beginner-friendly guide to hybrid cloud strategies.

- **"Architecting the Cloud"** by Michael J. Kavis: Insights into cloud design and architecture.

- Follow publications like **InfoWorld** and **TechCrunch** for the latest hybrid cloud news.

---

6. Open-Source Projects

Explore and contribute to open-source projects:

- **Kubernetes:** Container orchestration for hybrid cloud.

- **Terraform:** Infrastructure as Code (IaC) for hybrid cloud environments.

- **Prometheus:** Monitoring and alerting toolkit.

Final Thoughts

Hybrid cloud technology has emerged as a transformative solution for modern organizations, offering the flexibility to adapt to evolving business needs while ensuring security, scalability, and cost efficiency. The key to success lies in continuous learning, strategic planning, and collaboration across teams.

As you embark on your hybrid cloud journey, remember that challenges are opportunities for growth. Experiment, innovate, and build solutions that align with your organization's unique goals and aspirations. With the knowledge and skills gained from this guide, you are well-equipped to lead in the dynamic world of hybrid cloud computing.

Next Steps:

1. Apply what you've learned by designing a pilot hybrid cloud project.

2. Explore advanced topics like AI integration, edge computing, and multi-cloud orchestration.

3. Stay informed about emerging technologies and adapt your strategies accordingly.

Your hybrid cloud journey begins here—embrace the possibilities, and shape the future of IT.

www.ingramcontent.com/pod-product-compliance
Lightning Source LLC
La Vergne TN
LVHW022337060326
832902LV00022B/4098